HORSE CONTROL
— THE RIDER

TOM ROBERTS

HORSE CONTROL — THE RIDER

© TOM ROBERTS 1980
2nd Edition 1982

National Library of Australia card number and ISBN
0 9599413 2 0

Should be read after or in conjunction with:
"HORSE CONTROL AND THE BIT"

1st Edition 1971
2nd Edition 1973
3rd Edition 1975
4th Edition 1977
5th Edition 1979
6th Edition 1982

"HORSE CONTROL — THE YOUNG HORSE"
[The Handling, Breaking-in and Early Schooling
of Your Own Young Horse]

1st Edition 1974
2nd Edition 1977
3rd Edition 1979

Published by T.A. & P.R. Roberts,
241 West Beach Road, Richmond, South Australia. 5033.

Type-setting by Tilbrook Bros. — 'Northern Argus'
Clare, South Australia. 5453.

Printed by Stock Journal Publishers Pty Ltd
Adelaide, South Australia.

In 1949 the author, on Miss D. Marsom's "Elkedra", demonstrates a Flying Change of Leg to an audience of interested riders in Adelaide, South Australia. The Dressage Club of South Australia was formed soon afterwards and many of the onlookers became Foundation Members of the Club — the first of its kind in Australia.

ACKNOWLEDGEMENTS

First and foremost I would like to acknowledge my indebtedness to the late Mr FRANZ MAIRINGER for his help, advice and so skilful instruction. In this work I am able to quote him repeatedly. When I was in hospital for a long period he visited me and read the draft of a good many of the chapters. The fact that he showed approval and offered no criticism I found most encouraging. Thanks again to Franz, and his help over so many years.

Many thanks, too, to the hospital nursing staff who facilitated my efforts to recover and to write.

Miss KAY IRVING, B.A., M.B.E., is another who has inspired and helped me over the years. We have much to say about Kay on other pages but I take pleasure in thanking her again for her help and her so consistent reading and re-reading of the MSS.

Many thanks too, to Miss Rita Quorn-Smith for her many sketches — for which she would accept no fee. Rita's speciality is the loading of horses reluctant to go on to transport: thanks again Rita for your efforts with the pen.

The photographs are mostly the work of Mr Ian Roddie, and what a difficult task it proved to be. To get photos is easy; to get the exact time and angle — and weather — is anything but easy. Many thanks, Ian. A few of the photographs have come from other sources and where we have been able to do so we show the photographer's name and thank them.

Once again I have to pass my warmest thanks to my Dear Wife, Pat, and this is by no means a formality. So often Pat has made suggestions that not only improve the work — but their inclusion often means much retyping. Pat keeps it all fun.

To Dear Pat, my warmest possible thanks.

CONTENTS

LIST OF ILLUSTRATIONS

FRONTISPIECE:
In 1949 the author demonstrates a 'Flying Change of Leg' on Miss D. Mansom's "Elkedra" to an interested audience.

INTRODUCTION

Although it is the rider I have in mind in this work, I have repeatedly to refer readers to my first two books which deal with the education and control of the horse. I strongly recommend the reading of both "HORSE CONTROL AND THE BIT" and "HORSE CONTROL — THE YOUNG HORSE" — and then this: "HORSE CONTROL — THE RIDER".

Throughout the pages of this book I repeatedly stress the importance of the basic guidelines of horse education: the avoidance of punishment while encouraging the precept "That will profit you" or "That will profit you not".

One of the earliest chapters deals with the discovery in 1887 of what is known today as the 'Forward Seat", which led to shorter stirrups being used in most riding tasks.

A most important chapter is Chapter 9, which deals with "The Control of the Head and Neck". Before we think to advance our horse's education to the point where he carries himself with the balance and elegance of collection, we should have taught him to lower and lengthen his neck to our command. The more impulsive the horse the more important it is that we teach him to 'take rein' and lengthen his stride. THIS IS A MOST IMPORTANT EARLY LESSON.

No attempt is made to cover every aspect of dressage — but I recommend a knowledge of dressage, if only as a means to an end. It gives us a progressive system of horse training — and we need go no further than suits our own purpose.

It is many years since I last rode in a dressage test but I have studied the ever-changing rules in detail. One of the latest changes has been the introduction of 'Leg-yielding', and Chapter 19 deals with this, the first of the lateral exercises. Note how each exercise leads us on to the next.

I have quoted the International Rules repeatedly, and if a rider is interested in dressage I recommend the purchase of a copy of the latest F.E.I. Rules. Whatever our sport, we should be completely at home with the rules.

Tom Roberts

HORSE CONTROL — THE RIDER

TOM ROBERTS

CHAPTER 1

THE ADVENT OF THE MOTOR CAR
AND THE ADOPTION OF THE FORWARD SEAT

Necessity to keep horses serviceable;
Balance of the horse;
Accidental discovery of the 'forward seat';
The show-jumping seat and its evolution;
A different seat for a different task.

NECESSITY TO KEEP HORSES SERVICEABLE

Prior to the 20th Century a first essential in a horse was a long life of useful service to man.

In those days, every effort was made to keep horses sound and active and it was commonplace for a horse to be in constant work up to 25 years of age and even more.

The damage that can be done to a horse's legs if he is used for hard work or fast work or constant work before he is fully matured, was recognised by all. To start and keep a young horse in hard work a year or so before he reaches his sixth year often results in the loss of a dozen years at the other end of his life, and this fact was very well known.

Just to start the breaking-in and early schooling of a young horse as a two-three or four year-old is quite a sound practice providing we keep in mind that *he will not be sufficently matured for constant hard or fast work much before he reaches his sixth year.* In the days of cavalry for instance, the British Army would not accept a 4-year-old horse even as a gift. Five years was the minimum age, and during his fifth year the horse was slowly and carefully conditioned to the demands that might be made on him at six years and after.

Many studs in those days made a practice of having fillies broken-in during their third year, and they were then put to horse and carried a foal during their third-fourth year. This aimed to cut costs and it also did much to ensure foal-bearing quite late in the mare's life.

Today we often have youngsters racing at two and three years of age and

1

they are often broken-down with their useful life finished before they are five years old.

A century ago races of 5 to 50 miles were anything but uncommon, yet the history of the Thoroughbred shows many of the greatest horses of their times were still racing and winning at 25 years of age. The late start in life had much to do with this. No knowledgeable horseman risked the horse's legs to save a few months' keep in his early years.

THE GREAT CHANGES BROUGHT ABOUT BY THE MOTOR CAR

The horse was the main means of transport in those days and he had to be serviceable, wear-resistant and reliable.

It might be easier for you to understand what this implies if I quote from a very old South Australian Police File. It tells how a Mounted Constable was sent off at less than 24 hours' notice on a journey of well over a thousand miles — and return — on his Police Horse through almost uninhabited country (see Fig. 1). Here's the story.

On one Sunday afternoon in 1855 the following message was casually delivered:

"TO MOUNTED CONSTABLE WHITE (I have forgotten the actual names): "You will proceed tomorrow, Monday . . . , to Barrow Creek where upon arrival you will relieve Mounted Constable Black to permit him to proceed to Darwin to explain why he has not refunded the sum of five pounds he was overpaid early in 1854. You will take Police Mare Constance."

At 24 hours' notice each of these Troopers was sent off on a journey of thousands of miles. Between them they actually traversed the Continent of Australia from its southern coast to its northern coast — and return — to recover five pounds. No preliminary notice was given nor was it expected to be given. In each case the means of transport was the Constable's *ordinary every-day mount.* It was not until many many months later that Mounted Constable White arrived back at the Police Barracks in Adelaide.

A very interesting file I found it: and it serves to bring home to us how the role of the horse has changed since the advent of the motor-car.

The sequel to the above adds to the File's interest: by the time Mounted Constable Black reached Darwin, proof had arrived (by ship) that the five pounds had been refunded . . . and had been received in Adelaide some weeks after Mounted Constable White had departed.

The file is now in the State Archives and I merely quote it here as an indication of the demands likely, and expected, to be made on a horse prior to the motor-car and railway — and in this case, before the overland telegraph had made its appearance.

It takes seven years to bring the horse from conception to full maturity and full usefulness. His useful life needed to be at least three times that length to make him a sound financial proposition. Full hard work was avoided, if possible, until the horse was six years old.

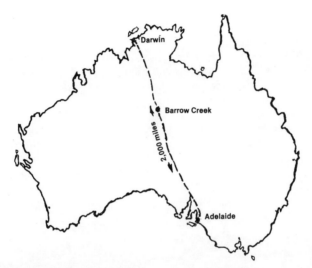

Fig. 1
THE HORSE IN THE 19TH CENTURY
Before the installation of the Overland Telegraph, a Mounted Police Constable was ordered to take his ordinary Police Mount and proceed from Adelaide to Barrow Creek in the Northern Territory of Australia. There he relieved another Mounted Constable who had then to proceed to Darwin.
The total distance travelled by the two men was just over four thousand miles.

ANOTHER GREAT CHANGE WAS THE ADOPTION OF THE FORWARD SEAT

Why did all riders sit so differently prior to the 20th Century? They seldom, if ever, leaned forward in the saddle.

> *Their aim was, among other things, to prolong the horse's useful life.*

BALANCE OF THE HORSE

Over the centuries it has been clearly proven that an excess of weight carried on the horse's forehand damages the forelegs.

This damage occurs mostly in the lower leg and is caused by the force with which the forefoot repeatedly strikes the ground at faster paces. The faster the pace at which the horse travels and the more weight he is carrying as the forefoot strikes the ground, the greater the damage caused by the concussion, particularly if the horse is moving on hard ground. The more immature the horse, the easier and

3

earlier he 'breaks down' and the more permanent the effects.

The balance of the horse — the proportion of weight carried on the forehand as compared with that carried on the hindquarters — has always been a major concern. Even an unridden horse normally carries about two-thirds of his weight on his forehand. This disparity is increased when the horse is ridden, as the weight of the rider and the saddle is also carried on the forepart of the horse's barrel and close to the forelegs.

> *The way the rider sat and his position in the saddle, as well as the length of stirrup used, all aimed at placing the weight further back and off the forehand — it saved the horse's forelegs. For the same reason the rider never leaned forward even when jumping or race-riding.*

In addition to the matter of the wear and tear on the forelegs, it is a fact that the better balanced the horse is the quicker he can stop and turn, so every effort was made in the various Riding (or Dressage) Schools of Europe to lighten the forehand. It not only extended the useful life of the horse but it also increased his handiness in battle, sport and display.

Fig. 2
To lighten the forehand and so prolong the horse's useful life, riders leaned back when jumping. Note the careful light contact with the horses' mouths — despite the awkward looking seat to today's eyes.

From an old print: "Steeplechasing"

Even in England where dressage was not popular, prior to the 20th Century both the very long stirrup and the upright seat were used on the racecourse and in the hunting field. To lean back when jumping a fence was the universal practice (see Fig. 2).

We find, then, that over the centuries — right up until about 1890 — horsemen all over the world rode to lighten the forehand and 'balance' the horse. The aim was to have the hindquarters carry as much weight as possible because it definitely lengthened the useful life of the horse.

4

What — then — caused the great changes during the last decade of the 19th Century . . . and thereafter?

THE ACCIDENTAL DISCOVERY OF THE 'FORWARD SEAT'

DISCOVERY THAT A HORSE GALLOPED FASTER AND JUMPED BETTER WITH THE RIDER 'FORWARD' ALONG HIS NECK

Two things happened just before the turn of the century that led to the big changes of today. They were:

. . . the accidental discovery of the 'forward seat' and
. . . the advent of the motor car.

An incident in the United States of America in about the year 1887 revolutionised the racing seat and led to the discovery that a horse could gallop faster and jump both higher and longer with the rider's weight well forward, either over the withers or even further forward, over the neck.

Here, briefly, is what happened. About the year stated a young horse of no particular merit was entered for a local race. At the last moment the jockey engaged to ride him proved unavailable and it was eventually decided to let the youngster have his first gallop under one of the stable boys.

To the astonishment of all the horse won the race in record time, 'Notwithstanding' — to quote the local paper — "the black boy crouched forward along the horse's neck like a monkey on a stick."

It appeared from this that the stable had a wonder-horse. However, although in subsequent races the horse was ridden by the best jockeys obtainable, he failed to show anything of his first brilliance.

Disappointed, and after much talk and speculation, the owner again raced the horse under the stable boy who perched up on his neck. Again the horse won his race by a great margin.

It now seemed clear that the increase of pace was in some way associated with the rider, possibly — although almost incredibly — in the way he crouched along the horse's neck like a monkey.

The details do not matter today perhaps, but subsequent tests and measurements proved that with shorter stirrups and with the rider perched well forward over the withers and neck, the horse galloped all distances in much better time. Moveover, measurements showed that each galloping stride was definitely longer than when the jockey sat upright in the established manner.

It is hard today to imagine the furore this discovery created.

5

The incident led to the advantages of the forward seat with its shorter stirrup being forced upon the racing world of the United States and a few years later a jockey — Tod Sloan — introduced it into England. There, for many years, it was known as the 'Tod Sloan Seat' or the 'Tod Sloan Crouch'.

As was to be expected, the innovation met with tremendous opposition in both countries. Some racehorse trainers and owners refused to admit the advantages of the 'forward seat', kept to the old 'balanced seat', would not change and were eventually forced out of business.

The additional weight on the forehand might shorten the useful life of a horse . . . but the forward seat for racing was here to stay.

THE SHOW-JUMPING SEAT AND ITS EVOLUTION

Although measurements had shown that each stride or leap of a galloping horse was clearly lengthened by the forward seat, it was not until some ten or more years later that an Italian Cavalry Officer, Capt. Frederico Caprilli, tried and proved the advantages of the forward seat when jumping.

As with racing, the forward seat for jumping and for cross-country riding met with great opposition, particularly from the English who felt it would damage their horse's legs. Many fox-hunters never did accept the forward seat although by 1914, when the writer joined the British Army, a modified forward seat was firmly established there.

Eventually the continued overwhelming successes of the Italians in International Jumping Competitions forced recognition of the advantages of the Italian Forward Jumping Seat upon the world. Long, long after this, however, there were those in the hunting field still riding with the upright seat and very long stirrups. This explains why 'the English Hunting Saddle' was specified as the only type allowed in the International Rules for Dressage Events.

I'll have more to say about the evolution of the Show-jumping seat in Chapter 24.

SHOW-JUMPING SEAT NOT SUITED FOR HUNTING

I am only concerned here and now to draw your attention to the fact that changes are still taking place in the modern show-jumping seat. There are good reasons for these changes not being extended to the hunting field.

In today's show-jumping with its big prize money, safety is certainly not a major consideration.

With so short a stirrup, the rider does not expect to stay with his horse if things go wrong. He is out to win — and safety and comfort become secondary considerations.

DIFFERENT SEAT FOR DIFFERENT TASK

Today, a knowledgeable rider will change his seat and length of stirrup to fit in with the purposes he has in mind on any particular occasion. Riding dressage, we will be most concerned with sitting balanced and relaxed. The rider usually takes a long stirrup to be able to sit as 'deep' in the saddle as possible and to balance the combined weight of horse and rider between fore and hind legs.

For hunting and similar tasks we would do well to use the Caprilli seat with its moderately short stirrups, and riding stock-work we might let our leathers out a hole or two further. Neither the very long stirrup of dressage nor the very short stirrup of show-jumping is quite as secure or as comfortable as the intermediate length.

It is most important that riders use a saddle designed for the purpose they have in mind — and in the next chapter I have something to say about the effects produced by different types of saddle.

CHAPTER 2

SELECTING A DRESSAGE OR HACKING SADDLE

Saddles — why does your saddle seat have a waist?
A good dressage or hacking saddle makes it easier
*   to sit in the correct place;*
Avoid anything that tends to increase the spread of
*   the saddle under the rider's leg;*
F.E.I. Rules.

SADDLES — AND RIDERS — START WITH THE SEAT

Sitting correctly will be easier if we start with a suitable saddle: a saddle designed for the type of riding we are about to follow.

In racing, show-jumping and cross-country riding, the rider of today stands in his stirrups at the critical moments of his ride. Saddles for these purposes are not designed to sit 'in' *but for standing or 'perching' in.*

Non-jumping saddles such as those required for dressage, hacking and stock-work, should be designed to SIT in. Others, such as the hunting saddle, should be designed and cut to serve both purposes easily and comfortably.

In 'sitting' saddles — dressage, hacking etc. — the seat itself is perhaps the most important part.

Fig. 3

Miss Barbara Marsden of 'Anahdale', Blayney, N.S.W., shows her well-proven Australian stock-saddle. Note the packing under the cantle which sits the rider well forward into the waist of the saddle. Note, too, the stockman's method of fitting the stirrup and leather [shown in detail on p. 34 of 'Horse Control —The Young Horse').
A comfortable saddle for both horse and rider is a necessity on a large station property.

8

WHY DOES THE SEAT HAVE A WAIST?

You will surely have noticed that the seat of your saddle has a distinct 'waist' . . . that is, a marked narrowing towards the front part of the centre of the seat. To form the waist, both the seat of the saddle and the side-bars of the saddle-tree on which the saddle is built, are narrowed to accommodate the rider's fork. When the rider sits close to the waist he finds this narrowing of the seat allows his legs to drop easily and comfortably when he rides with a longer stirrup.

The longer the stirrup to be used the more important it is that the rider sits well *INTO* the waist.

With this in mind, we should check to see that the lowest part of the saddle WHEN IT IS ON THE HORSE'S BACK is only just behind the waist. Gravity will always tend to shake the rider down into the lowest part of the seat when he sits relaxed, as he should.

I stress this point as it is important that the design and construction of a good hacking, dressage or stock saddle is such that it is easy to sit in the best place — well forward close to the waist. There is only one place to check the saddle for this feature — and that is when it is on the horse's back, on the horse on which it is to be used.

A GOOD DRESSAGE OR HACKING SADDLE MAKES IT EASIER TO SIT IN THE CORRECT PLACE

For many years there was a marked tendancy to put excessive packing under the front part of the saddle — each side of the pommel and under the saddle flap — and an equally marked tendancy to reduce the amount of packing under the rear part of the saddle, the cantle. This often resulted in the lowest part of the seat being much further back than it should have been. Today, however, most saddlers have corrected this serious fault.

Notice the thickness of the packing at the back of the old and proven stock saddles (and there are still many about today, see Fig. 3). The rider just CANNOT sit on the back of a good stock saddle; its design (its high back) compels him to sit well forward and down — just behind the waist of the seat. Although we do not need the high cantle of a stock saddle when hacking or in dressage, it is important that we are not compelled to fight gravity in order to keep our seat in the correct place: forward, in or near the waist.

You may ask: "Why is the back part of the saddle always made so wide if not for the rider to sit on?"

A good question.

The additional width is there *to enable the rider's weight to be spread over a large area of the horse's back.* Remember, the saddle-tree has been narrowed to form the 'waist' and needs to be widened again to compensate for the reduced area

9

over which the rider's weight presses due to this narrowing.

Never forget the final rule of saddle fitting (read again Chapter 2, 'HORSE CONTROL AND THE BIT') —

> "The whole of the weight should be evenly distributed over the ribs through the medium of the muscles covering them."

The extra spread at the back of the saddle is for the benefit of the horse and is most essential for his comfort — and if a sore back from long or regular riding is to be avoided.

SIT 'DEEP'

To 'sit deep' means that the rider sits with his knees as far down as possible, while his stirrup irons maintain their proper position immediately under the saddle stirrup-dee. *The stirrup leather should hang vertically* so as to permit it to carry the rider's weight when he wants to stand or perch — or just lift saddle.

A shorter stirrup allows the rider's knee to be taken more forward so that he can balance or perch *over* his knees when he is actually doing the task he aims to do. A flat-race jockey moving his horse about before his race usually sits *on* his saddle; we often see his shins absolutely perpendicular and his seat well back at the rear of the saddle. *But not during his race.*

No matter how long or how short the stirrup used, the rider should sit as 'deep' as is possible with the length of stirrup he has. This will mean that as the stirrup used gets shorter and shorter, the knee will be taken further and further forward. As the knee goes forward the rider's shin-bones more and more approach the horizontal when he rides at the work he is asking of his horse: hunting, eventing, show-jumping or racing, etc.

AVOID ANYTHING THAT TENDS TO INCREASE THE SPREAD OF THE SADDLE UNDER THE RIDER'S LEG

We have shown how the seat and saddle-tree is narrowed into a waist to reduce the spread at the rider's fork. The best saddle-makers take this matter further and also do all they can to allow the rider's knees and thighs to lie as close to the horse as possible. Every effort should be made not to cause protuberances a little further down — under the saddle-flaps.

Girth buckles can be a real nuisance when they make a bump that can be felt under the rider's leg. To avoid this completely, we find that today a number of good dressage saddles have a girth strap made very long and fitted with girths correspondingly short, so that the buckles lie well below the saddle-flaps: in some instances higher than the horse's elbow and in others well below the elbow. This

Fig. 4
Mrs D. Batten shows us the long
girth straps and short girth of her
dressage saddle on Miss M.
Goode's "Spring Song".
As is usual with a dressage-only
saddle, it is not intended to be
used with a short stirrup.

solves the problem of bulky girth-buckles which, if sited under the flap, can and often do, increase the spread of horse and saddle (see Fig. 4).

When the saddle is fitted with the normal much shorter girth straps and long girth, we should see that the length of the girth is such as to allow the buckles to lie where they will least interfere with the rider's legs and knees.

Check, too, that the girth is adjusted so that the buckles are at *the same level* each side of the horse. The saddle should feel the same under each thigh. If the saddle has to be used on several horses, it is sometimes an advantage to have girths of different lengths so that the buckles will lie at about the same level on each side.

Each matter is a trifle on its own, but together they affect the rider's appearance, seat and the judge's marks in a dressage test. It is not so important when jumping or racing, where the knee is taken more forward and is in front of the girth straps and buckles.

GIRTHS — FITZWILLIAM

If you use a Fitzwilliam girth, check to see that the buckle on the central shorter girth strap does not ride over the top of any part of the other two buckles, thus doubling the size of the bump under the saddle-flap. It is to AVOID this happening that the centre girth should be made *at least two buckle-lengths shorter* than the main girth of a Fitzwilliam. Check to see that the centre girth is short enough to prevent this 'doubling up' (see Fig. 5).

BUCKLES

The best girth buckles are, or were, themselves designed to reduce to a minimum any bump or lump they necessarily create under the saddle-flap. A first-class girth buckle used to be so cleverly and carefully made that the tongue

11

of the buckle did not project higher than the part of the buckle it rested upon.

Very few, if any, buckles comply with this requirement today, so saddlers find it necessary to place another piece of leather *over the buckle* to protect the underside of the saddle-flap from the tip of the tongue of the girth-buckle. This additional piece of leather adds a little more to the spread each side under the rider's legs: first the buckle, then the tongue of the buckle — and then the piece of leather needed to protect the saddle from the protruding tongue.

Again, trifles. But they didn't consider them so in the old 'horse days'.

Fig. 5
Fitzwilliam Girth Buckles
The centre overlapping strap should be a full buckle length shorter than the other buckles, on each side of the saddle.
If the centre girth is made too long its buckles lie on the others and increase the bump under the rider's knees.
If the centre girth is made a little shorter, no harm is done.

BULKY SADDLE-CLOTHS

If a bulky saddle-cloth such as a sheepskin is used under the saddle-flap it adds even more to the spread under the rider. It serves no useful purpose, for the horse needs no protection there. On the contrary, in dressage we want our horse to feel the slightest additional pressure of our legs when we use them: how inconsistent to add the bulk of a sheepskin saddle-cloth to protect him from our legs, and then perhaps have to use spurs on him a little lower down his side.

True, the Spanish Riding School in Vienna uses a saddle cloth; a large one, but not a thick one. Its purpose is to protect the long tails of the rider's coat from the horse.

The competition dressage and hack rider should at least know of these matters, for they affect the appearance of the rider and are often reflected in the decisions of the judge. Sitting close to the horse does help, and there is much to be said for the very short girths with girth buckles well below the saddle-flaps, just slightly below or slightly above the horse's elbows. It must be seen, of course, that there is no interference with the elbow itself.

Have as little as possible between your thigh-bones and your horse.

I have just been cautioning you against having heavy packing under the saddle-flap — not packing under the saddle-TREE, the weight-bearing part of the saddle. There, a sheepskin may well add to the horse's comfort without in any way spreading the rider's knees.

F.E.I. RULES FOR DRESSAGE EVENTS 1979

Article 432 — Saddlery

[1] The following are compulsory: English saddle, double bridle, i.e. bit and bridoon with curb chain. Lipstrap and rubber or leather cover for curb chain are optional.

[2] Martingales, any kind of gadgets [such as bearing, side, running or balancing reins, etc.], any kind of boots or bandages and any form of blinkers are, under penalty of elimination, strictly forbidden.

WHY ENGLISH SADDLE?

The old type of English saddle was designed and was well-suited *for riding with long stirrups,* even when hunting, and that of course necessitated a long and straightish leg. Well before the mid-twenties the Army and the more advanced riders in England had recognised and were using the modern forward seat with the shorter stirrup, and with it a more forward-cut saddle flap. The hunting fraternity, however, were generally much more conservative and a great many still kept to the long stirrup and the old type of saddle.

WHY DID THE ENGLISH PREFER HUNTING TO DRESSAGE?

Of course there is a good reason.

In winter on the Continent of Europe the ground is so cold — often frozen hard — that outdoor riding is almost impossible except on specially prepared ground. Anything like hunting was, and is, out of the question during the very cold months.

The coasts of England and Ireland, however, are surrounded by the warmer waters of the Gulf Stream and the ground is frozen only occasionally. Hunting, with its exhilarating cross-country gallops, is possible most of the winter and horsemen and women all over those countries took part.

On the Continent, enclosed riding schools or arenas became very popular

13

and the gentry spent most of the mornings at least, there. It is easy to imagine how things went in those usually crowded arenas and how, with the ladies looking on from the galleries, great competition resulted: and how each rider would vie with the other in taking his horse's accomplishments beyond the others. Dressage was considered an art rather than utility.

The English did not need the schools except for Military training. They preferred their hunting — and certainly did nothing to encourage dressage.

I can quite well imagine the Continental dressage riders agreeing that the English Hunting Saddle, which had not changed with the times, would do very nicely as a model suited for dressage riding. The decision was probably not meant to be a compliment.

'Maybe this' and 'maybe that', but there is nothing in the Dressage Rules to justify a judge demanding a very long stirrup. On the other hand, the ease and grace of the expert with a long stirrup and its complete absence of stiffness and effort, might wring an extra mark or so from the toughest judge.

TO SUM UP

A first class dressage or hacking saddle will assist in elegant and effortless riding, but it is quite unsuited for racing, show-jumping, etc.

It is of the utmost importance that the horse should find the saddle comfortable [see pp. 8-9 'HORSE CONTROL AND THE BIT' for rules of saddle fitting]. A well-designed saddle will be comfortable for the horse as well as helpful to the rider.

To enable the rider to sit evenly and easily, the first requirement of a dressage or hacking saddle is that the lowest part of the seat is close to the waist of the saddle **when it is on the horse's back and the rider seated.** If you sit further back you will be riding at a definite disadvantage — or if competition riding, you will be giving your competitors a definite advantage.

Avoid bumps and protuberance under the saddle flaps. Have nothing under the saddle flaps that will increase the spread of the horse.

CHAPTER 3

PART I : PART II

THE CORRECT DRESSAGE SEAT

Disadvantages of incorrect seat;
'Seat' starts at the seat of the saddle.

PART I: AT SEAT LEVEL AND BELOW

Sit close to the saddle;
International Rules for Dressage Seat;
'Every effect creates an opposite and equal effect';
Position of the foot.

PART II: AT SEAT LEVEL AND ABOVE

'Down the weight — Upright the body';
'Sit tall in the saddle';
Position of arms and hands;
Height of hands when holding the reins;
Position of the hands;
Position of the eyes;
De-contraction;
When instructing.

The term 'seat' in its broadest application includes the position of the body, the arms, legs, head — and eyes. It also includes the condition of our muscles: are we sitting stiffly or relaxed?

Indeed, it might well be said that the *relaxed condition of our muscles* is the most important factor whether the seat be for dressage, racing, jumping or games.

There are many points upon which the various schools of dressage differ: but they all agree on the importance of the seat. Moreover, all seem to agree as to what IS the 'correct' seat.

DISADVANTAGES OF AN INCORRECT SEAT

Now — instead of starting off to tell you of the many advantages of the correct seat, I'm going to reverse that procedure and first set out the DISADVANTAGES linked with OTHER than the correct seat.

Every sport has a basic position from which the participant is recommended to work: golfing, fencing, boxing etc. Each has its 'correct' stance or position and we might do well to note the great care and attention the players give to this.

Could anyone for instance be more fussy about his position, his balance, or his muscular condition than a top golfer? You must have watched with wonder at first at the careful placing of his feet — then the testing and checking for looseness in his swing — as such a golfer prepares to hit off. Again and again he adjusts the placing of his feet and body BEFORE he actually plays the ball. Notice, too, how he makes several trial swings to check against the slightest stiffness.

In riding as with every sport, any position OTHER than the correct or approved position will be found to have some disadvantage or other. The correct position is accepted as the best because it will have been **proved** that any other will put the player at some disadvantage. This is the point I wish to stress.

The correct seat for any form of riding will not give you an advantage over another rider who also sits correctly — but any seat OTHER than the correct seat will put you at a disadvantage.

In any riding competition you will improve the other fellow's chances if you sit *other* than correctly . . . and your 'seat' begins at the seat of the saddle.

Fig. 6
Gayle Hutchens shows us an ideal seat position — and quite unconscious of the camera. A vertical line from head to heel would pass through the hips. State Titles 1979, Dressage Association of South Australia.

PART I

POSITION OF THE BODY AT SEAT LEVEL AND BELOW

As I have already said: 'First sit down into the waist of your saddle'. If you have followed the advice given on the selection of a saddle, this will be easy as the waist will be the lowest and narrowest part of the seat and so gravity will help you stay there.

If, when sitting in the correct place, you allow your legs to drop as far as they will drop without stirrups, you will find that friction from the saddle will interfere with them dropping straight down. To get them to drop down as far as they can go down, you will need to take each leg off the saddle — take knees and thighs clear of contact — and THEN let them drop.

When you have done this correctly, you will find your knees will hang just about directly under your hip-joint — but your toes and knees will both be pointing well outward. You will also note a sizeable muscle or wad of flesh between the thigh-bone and the saddle, and this too will be keeping your thigh-bones and knees away from the saddle. To correct this, you should now roll or turn the thighs and knees so that the front of each knee points to your front instead of outwards. To do this, you will have to revolve each thigh-bone in its socket at the hip.

Have you the idea? Turn each thigh-bone, revolve it at the hip socket joint so as to roll the front of the knee towards your front.

Your next move is to carry your knees forward a little, bending your leg at the knee as you do so to keep the foot about under the hip joint.

SIT CLOSE TO THE SADDLE

This first dropping the legs down and then raising the knees and rolling the front of the knee in toward the saddle will effectively draw or push that wad of flesh or muscle back from the inside of the thigh, thus allowing your thigh-bone to lie much closer to your saddle.

But . . . however you do it . . . do displace this flesh or muscle to the rear so that you can sit with your thigh-bones close to your horse. Some riders just put a hand under the back of the thigh and pull the muscles back out of the way; others take a leg off the saddle as I have described, let the leg drop down and then carry it forward into position.

Reducing the spread and getting 'as close to your horse as you can' is a first essential. Not only will you be able to contact your horse more easily, but by allowing you to sit deeper *it greatly improves your appearance.*

With your toes raised you will now have your legs in about the recommended position. Adjust the stirrups to this length or perhaps a little shorter if for any reason you prefer to do so, and then just put your feet into the irons.

When you have your foot in the stirrup, let the leg, the heel, hang down relaxed into the iron. The front of each knee should at all times be rolled to point towards the front; the thigh, knee and the top of each shinbone should all lie in light contact with the saddle (see Fig. 7).

Fig. 7
Positioning the lower part of the leg and the thigh, and giving special attention to the 'calf' of the leg. The knee and heel well down and the leg correctly placed. We are not attending to the hands and arms at the moment. A young Jody Sitters of Glenalta on her first pony, "Smokey".

OFF-SET STIRRUP IRONS

These stirrups have much to be said for them so I will add something about the irons — so often wrongly used through having been placed on the incorrect side of the saddle.

The dee in the stirrup iron itself is placed a little to one side of the centre, and another difference is that the tread of the stirrup is not made level — it slopes.

The purpose of the sloping tread is to make it easy to keep the heel down lower than the toe — that's easily seen — but quite a few riders think the off-set dee is meant to lower the outside of the iron and the outside of the rider's foot.

This is not so. **It is the outside of the rider's foot that should be raised,** and the stirrup iron should be fitted to the saddle so that it raises the rider's little toe a fraction higher than the big toe (see Fig. 8). An onlooker or instructor should normally be able to see something of the sole of the rider's boot.

The foot, so placed, tends to push the rider's knee in against the saddle, and so increases the contact of the legs without muscular effort. [Right now you can prove the truth of this. Stand up with your knees well bent and apart, and then raise your little toes.)

Fig. 8
OFF-SET STIRRUP IRON
When placed on the saddle correctly, as shown, the slope on the stirrup-tread encourages the heel to drop and the 'off-set' raises the little toe higher than the big toe. Read the last two paras. above which explain 'why'.
Miss Kerry Mack showing us her stirrup at the Club Grounds.

INTERNATIONAL RULES FOR DRESSAGE SEAT

Rule No. 417 deals with the 'Position of the Rider', and the following is all that it has to say about the position and condition of the rider's legs:

> "He [the rider] should be well balanced, with his loins and hips supple, thighs and legs steady and well stretched downwards."

Nothing there about the *length* of stirrup, and today since Combined Training Events have become so popular there is a growing tendency to accept a somewhat shorter stirrup as not necessarily disadvantageous for dressage.

The dressage seat with its extremely long stirrup has been in existence for centuries. The advantages of a short stirrup were not proved until about the 1890's. It is true the very short stirrup does not hold the advantages in dressage

19

that it has in jumping and galloping — but is a somewhat shorter stirrup a disadvantage? I am sure it is not.

Look again at Rule 417 just quoted and I draw your attention to the fact that more attention is given to the *condition* than to the position, of the leg: "Well balanced with loins and hips supple: thighs and legs steady and well-stretched downwards".

The limbs with their muscles should be relaxed. With the muscles relaxed, the leg will drop and the stirrup will keep the toe up. The weight of the relaxed leg will stretch the heel well down.

'EVERY EFFECT CREATES AN OPPOSITE AND EQUAL EFFECT'

Do not force the heels down. The heel should not be pushed or forced down: it should *hang down*. Pushing downwards into the heel not only tenses the muscles, but it also has a lifting effect on the seat.

Remember the rule just quoted: "Thighs and legs steady and well-stretched downward". 'Stretched' — not forced — down.

Likewise, if you take your foot forward, pushing down and forward into the stirrup iron with your foot so placed, you will *definitely push your seat up and back*. Prove this for yourself as you sit in your chair. With your feet a little in front of you on the floor, press downward on to the floor and notice how this action will tend to push your seat, and your chair, to the rear and upward.

> *It might well be that this pushing of the foot forward*
> *and downward is the most serious of all the basic faults*
> *in the position of a dressage rider — and many others.*

It tenses the legs and parts of the body, and it is almost certain that the rider will not be AWARE that he is doing so. It is usually an unconcious happening that pushes the rider backward and upward and unknown to him **tightens the reins a little.** (The rider's arms go back with his body — and the horse gets the blame for starting to pull.)

Riding with the feet forward may not be a fault when riding stock or any other type of loose rein horsemanship; but it can cause a lot of trouble in dressage, where the position leads to a rider pushing back and so tightening the already lightly stretched rein used in dressage.

You will find, then, that there is good reason to advise 'do not press down hard on the stirrup'. Let the leg hang relaxed into the heel. If you are not gripping the saddle, and you should not be, the weight of the leg will be enough to depress the heel.

When the leg hangs relaxed into the stirrup you will find the toes will be higher than the heel: of course they will be. You don't walk with your heels higher than your toes, you let them drop to the ground. Let your heels drop too, when you have your feet in the stirrups. 'Heels up' is a sure sign of stiffness; if they are up, YOU are holding them up. Relax . . . let the weight of the relaxed leg depress the heel.

When you are using stirrups we say: 'Drop your heel'; only when not using a stirrup do we say: 'Raise your toes'.

The International Rules do not require the stirrup iron to be placed under any particular part of the foot, so we are at liberty to ride with the iron under the ball of the foot — which adds to our ease and balance — or the foot well home — or change from one positon to another.

POSITION OF THE FOOT

The foot is 'forward' when the stirrup leather, instead of dropping straight down so that the iron hangs immediately under the saddle stirrup-dee, is held to some extent in front of that line by the rider. If it is forward even to the slightest degree, you are holding — or pushing — it forward AND YOU ALMOST CERTAINLY WILL NOT KNOW YOU ARE DOING IT.

Again, it indicates stiffness.

I find that a dressage rider usually begins pushing his feet a little forward when his is riding a young horse. It is an almost certain indication that the rider is slightly nervous about the horse, even though he may not recognise the fact.

He will sit somewhat stiffly, pushing forward and down with his feet, and on the slightest provocation or imagined provocation he will increase the pressure and the stiffness. He does not recognise that he is now sitting constantly ready to hold — ready to pull. He is only too ready to apply the brakes — increase his hold on the reins — and usually does so unconciously. He will often use his heels the next second to counter the check he has unconciously asked from his horse.

At 76 I was still riding, but I found I had to watch my foot position very closely; any fall could well be serious. I had to be careful not to bring on the very thing I wanted to avoid.

With your upper leg in the recommended position and your heel relaxed and down, your foot should lie somewhat parallel to the horse's side.

TO SUM UP: PART I

Sit relaxed and down into the waist of the saddle, which should also be the lowest part of the seat of the saddle.

See that the thighs are well down, the knees rolled so as to point to the front, and the muscles on the inside of the thigh-bones drawn to the rear.

21

Allow the weight of your legs to depress your heels. Do NOT force your heels down or allow your foot to take the stirrup leather in front of the vertical.

Get your seat-bones and thigh-bones as close to the horse as is possible: but see that suppleness and relaxed condition are maintained.

PART II

POSITION OF THE BODY AT SEAT LEVEL AND ABOVE

'DOWN THE WEIGHT — UPRIGHT THE BODY'

We have shown how the legs should be stretched well down from the seat of the saddle and hang relaxed into the stirrup irons. Now we will find advantages in stretching the upper parts of the body in the opposite direction — upwards — with the rider sitting upright, straight, and balanced over the seat-bones.

SIT 'TALL IN THE SADDLE'

When we sit erect and balanced, little muscular effort is necessary to maintain that position. But any movement on the part of the horse will disturb this balance and we will then find it necessary to adjust our weight so that we can 'go with him'.

We have seen that when riding in racing and show-jumping etc., big changes in position become necessary; but in dressage it is only necessary to give our already balanced body a *minute* cant in the direction of movement — just a tiny angle to allow for or counter the influence of the horse's movement.

I have used the word 'cant' deliberately, for I want to avoid the word 'lean'. The tilt necessary is only a very small one, but I find many riders take 'lean' to such an exaggerated extent that it amounts to a definite fault.

Later on we will deal more fully with these small changes of balance for they assume great importance in dressage: they become an 'aid' which the horse learns to feel for and act upon.

'UPRIGHT THE BODY'

'Upright the body', commands Mr Franz Mairinger and other instructors and pupils of the Spanish Riding School in Vienna.

'Make the back long', exhorts the Dutch expert and instructor, Mr Berend van Eerton.

'He sits tall in the saddle', an admirer will say of a Western horseman.

22

Sit upright: sit tall: sit with a long body: all are different expressions from different countries and teachings but all are seeking and encouraging the same thing:

REACH UP . . STRETCH UP . . SIT BALANCED AND ERECT.

So first, sit down in your saddle with your seat well forward into the waist as already detailed. The seat position should always be checked before the body positon. Tell yourself:

> 1. *'Down the weight'*
>
> and 2. *'Upright the body'.*

With your weight well down on your seat-bones and your heels hanging well down in your stirrups, reach up *with the BACK of your head* as if you were trying to touch something, a measuring stick say, just out of reach.

You will find this ONE thought, this ONE effort, will:

> . . . straighten your back
> . . . set your shoulders back
> . . . take your chest forward and out
> . . . lift your head; and
> . . . tuck your chin in.

'Chin In' — trying to lift the *back* of the head will keep the chin *in*. Lifting the front of the head makes the chin stick out. We have more to say about this elewhere.

'Reaching up' will do wonders in improving your appearance — and not only when you are mounted on a horse. Sit up, reach up, look up — at all times, whether mounted or not.

It is not surprising that all schools of dressage agree: 'Upright the body'. The International Rules for Dressage, Rule 417 again, require:

> 'The upper part of the body easy, free and erect . . . with the arms close to the body . . .'.

Stretch up as if to touch, with the back of your head, something just out of reach. Remember: *the back of your head.*

> **'Down the weight'** . . . **on to the seat of the saddle.**
> **'Upright the body'** . . . **from the seat of the saddle.**

I need hardly say that if your weight is other than 'down', you are holding it up: you are *stiff*.

Fig. 9
Good horsemanship is the same whether astride or side-saddle. The rider sits relaxed, the body upright, the top of the hip well forward and the back of the head the highest part of the body. This photograph, taken 75 years ago, subscribes to all the rules of good horsemanship.

Pat's Grandmother, Mrs H. B. (Susan) Welch at the turn of the century on 'Panther'. A judge of the times was heard to comment: "If Mrs Welch rode a mule into the ring she would come out with the ribbon!" Sidesaddle events are becoming popular again today and those interested will notice the hairstyle, hat and veil; gloves (one not yet donned), and the skirt on the near side falls to the horse's girthline. Ladies in those days possessed 'limbs'. Legs and ankles were never mentioned — let alone seen! Photograph reproduced from an old and torn print by Mr Ian Roddie.

POSITION OF THE ARMS AND HANDS

Each upper arm should hang down lightly and relaxed from its shoulder joint. When so hanging, each elbow will be directly below its shoulder and will be lightly touching the rider's side.

The elbow should HANG in that position — not held either tightly against the side or away from the body. Neither should it lie in front of the shoulder-joint nor to the rear of that position.

If the elbow is pressed against the side or held out from the side, or positioned either in front of or behind the vertical line, then YOU are holding it

24

there. It indicates that you are stiff: using muscles unnecessarily and unconciously.

The elbows should hang loosely, directly under the shoulder-joint — until we want to use them.

Almost all judges approve, and show it, when the rider sits with his elbows well back, and even a little further back than when hanging immediately under the shoulder-joint.

Keep in mind that all these are basic positions: they are the positions from which it is most suitable to move or act, very much like the golfer's stance that we instanced earlier. This is particularly so with our hands. The height at which we hold our hands will be changing continually when we are riding, particularly when dealing with a young horse.

HEIGHT OF THE HANDS WHEN HOLDING THE REINS

The elbow remains hanging as already stated, and the hand is then raised by bending the arm at the elbow until — when viewed from the side — the forearm and rein would appear to run in a more or less straight line from the elbow to bit.

Note that I say: "When viewed from the side the line should appear about straight". It should certainly not appear anything like straight when the rider looks down from above.

Riders in their early years have often to be told to 'Lower your hands'; and being so continually admonished, this often leads them — and others — to think that the hands should be lower than I have recommended. A very low hand is a handicap when working a horse. Look at the next photograph you see of a first-class horseman, show-jumper, jockey, or dressage rider, and you will find that it is only occasionally that the height of the hands is other than stated above.

POSITIONING OF THE HANDS

With the hands at this height, they should be turned at the wrist so that the thumbs are uppermost. The wrists should then be somewhat bent so that the thumb-nails point more or less towards each other, some 2″—3″ (5cm) apart (see Fig. 10).

This means that each wrist will be bent in the same direction as the fingers are bent, and the wrists and the fingers will describe a relaxed quarter-circle (or perhaps a little less than that).

The bends in our elbows, wrists and fingers permit us to make the finer adjustments to the reins. At times the hands will be required to move considerably, and to do this the arms may need to be fully stretched out, as will, too, the wrists and fingers. All the joints in the arms, wrists, and fingers are somewhat flexed *in order to allow free movement in any direction.*

25

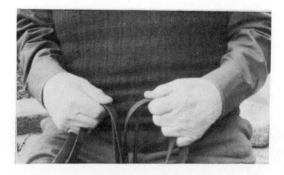

Fig. 10
I couldn't quite understand one instructor when he used the expression: "The thumbnails saying 'hello' to each other."
It proved to mean: Let your thumbnails face each other like two friends about to shake hands!

We should be able to give and take with our fingers . . . our hands . . . and our arms.

REINS IN ONE HAND

When riding with the reins in one hand and the other hand doing nothing, that is exactly what the unused hand should be doing — nothing. It should be allowed to hang straight down and like the elbow, the hand will then hang directly below its shoulder-joint.

The fingers, fully relaxed, should partly close the hand; the thumb should be to the front and the back of the hand should face to the outside. When your hand is not being used when you are mounted, it should do nothing, just hang. And when fully relaxed it will hang as described.

This is the position the hand should drop to in a dressage competition when the competitor salutes the judges.

[REINS: In Ch. 15 of 'HORSE CONTROL AND THE BIT', I have said a great deal about different kinds of reins: plaited, laced, covered, heavy or light reins . . . read it, for it is almost certain to be of help.]

POSITION OF THE EYES

Where you look when competition riding can be quite important.

The guide is: 'LOOK IN THE DIRECTION OF MOVEMENT'.

Very few do this when riding dressage unless they have been taught to do so. Most riders look down at their horse's head when riding in the manege. Discipline yourself not to do this.

LOOK UP . . . LOOK WELL UP . . . HIGH UP.

Make a practice of FEELING down — not looking down. You can feel a dozen things at one and the same time, whereas it is most difficult to see in more

26

than one direction. With practice, you can *feel* what each of your horse's limbs is doing in response to your hand and leg aids. You can also feel the *condition* of his head, neck and back muscles, whether they are relaxed and mobile, or stiff and rigid.

At best, looking down at the horse not only gives the onlooker the impression that your horse is fully engaging your attention: but is often associated with actual difficulty in managing him.

On the other hand, when the rider looks in the direction he is moving and well up, he appears to the onlooker or judge to be quite unconcerned about the horse he in controlling so easily.

> *Always look in the direction to which the horse is required to move.*

Looking in the direction of movement is particularly impressive in lateral (sideways) movements. In a half-pass, for instance, the rider should turn his head and shoulders — and look in the direction of movement. Even when horse and rider are moving in the direction of a nominated marker in the arena, the rider should not look at the marker but well above it — at a point some three metres above it. Make a point of looking up as well as in the direction of movement.

Aim to give the onlooker (or judge) the impression that the control of your horse hardly concerns you. Let them see that your horse not only - clearly understands what you want of him but that he takes pleasure in doing it . . . *and you can feel him doing it.*

DE-CONTRACTION

Once again: **"No position is a good one if the rider is in any way stiff".**

We must check, and check repeatedly, against stiffness. The best way of doing this is to deliberately use the muscles that operate the various parts of the body. For a second or two nod and twist your head a little, wriggle your shoulders and move your shoulder-blades on your back. Give your elbows a little flap or two and give your body a slight movement to either side — and do each of these things as exercise occasionally. You will find it is much easier to loosen a muscle if first you deliberately use it.

We used to call these little movements 'decontraction exercises'. It is hard to de-contract a muscle we have not first consciously contracted.

Remember at all times: looseness, or the absence of stiffness, is more important that any position. CHECK REPEATEDLY FOR LOOSENESS. Check that all your muscles are relaxed: 'Down the weight' and 'Upright the body'.

I have found it useful as a pupil made progress in his lessons to call his attention to the so-often repeated advice: 'Down the weight, upright the body', and the fact that the important word in each phrase is the first.

When he had made sufficient progress I would tell the pupil: "From now on I am only going to use the first word — you know quite well what follows. I'll say 'Down' and leave it to you to add 'the weight'."

A little later I would say: "Now, I want you to take this a little further. I'll just say 'Down' and leave it to you to complete: 'Down the weight *and upright the body'.*"

The rider should drop his weight, his seat, into the waist of the saddle and at the same time stretch upwards FROM the seat. We want him to do both things at the same time, and the pupil also realises that we recognise he is making definite progress.

Another pupil I once had, had never been able to straighten his back. He told me this repeatedly; then one day I asked him to stretch upwards — and the rounded back straightened immediately to the astonishment of each of us.

REACH UP. LOOK WHERE YOU ARE GOING, AND UP-WARDS. YOU WILL NOT ONLY IMPROVE YOUR RIDING BUT YOUR MOUNTED OR DISMOUNTED APPEARANCE!

☆   ☆   ☆

When instructing, we often find that putting a matter into different words is most effective.

In Poona, India, back in 1921, I was teaching a Spanish young lady to ride. Time after time after time, I said: "Signorina, lower your heels". "Drop your heels". "Let your heels drop lower than your toes . . .", but I could NOT get the message through.

Eventually I tried something different, and used the wrong instruction: "Signorina, please raise your toes."

The message although wrongly phrased had a wonderful effect. She immediately dropped her heel. 'Raising her toes' should have caused her to lift her foot off the stirrup iron — but she did as I wanted, and afterwards did as I wanted when requested this time to: "Lower your heels"!

This putting a thing a different way can be most useful in getting a message through to a difficult person with a horse, too. Keep it in mind.

TO SUM UP

"DOWN THE WEIGHT" . . . "UPRIGHT THE BODY"
"MAKE THE BACK LONG" . . . "SIT TALL IN THE SADDLE"
"LOOK UP — LOOK WELL UP OVER THE HORIZON"

And you will not only improve your riding but your whole appearance.

The forearms, wrists and fingers should more or less follow the contour of the body: thumbnails within an inch or two of each other and perhaps some two or three inches from the body.

The wrists should be rounded, with the backs of the fingers towards the front.

Viewed from the side, the hands should be inconspicuous. My old instructor would describe a stiff straight hand as a 'leg-of-mutton fist'. And do not ride as though 'pushing a pram'.

The correct position for hands, legs and body are only helpful as long as we are ready and able to move them quickly and smoothly — and with the exact delicacy or strength that meets the requirements of the moment.

Check and check again for stiffness. Seek lightness at all times; strength should seldom, if ever, be used.

Look well up and in the direction of movement: and let me remind you again to reach up as though trying to touch something with the BACK of your head, just out of reach. This will keep your chin *in* as you look up.

CHAPTER 4

THE INDEPENDENT SEAT AND THE AIDS

The independent seat;
What are the aids?
Lateral and diagonal 'effects'.

THE INDEPENDENT SEAT

The aids used on a trained dressage horse constitute a quite involved sort of sign language — something like the understanding that develops between good ballroom dancing partners.

The language of the aids, like the language of ballroom dancing, requires a constant contact between the partners by means of which each comes to *feel* what one requires of the other. An onlooker can neither see nor hear what each of the partners is able to detect so quickly, easily and accurately.

So it should be with horse and rider.

But before we can use our aids consistently, we have to develop a seat that leaves our hands and legs free and independent, permitting us to maintain our steady light contact with the horse — our partner.

In good horsemanship it is for the rider to pass on his requirements to his horse by the lightest and most delicate use of his body, hands, legs, and seat. All aids should be as light as possible.

It is clearly not possible for the rider to use consistently delicate and refined aids until he himself is quite secure in the saddle. His security must be quite independent of his limbs. This is what is meant by 'an independent seat'.

An independent seat is one that gives the utmost security and steadiness in the saddle, while leaving the rider's limbs and weight of his body free . . . first to control the horse and then for any purpose he might have in mind: for instance to use a polo stick or stockwhip, or to lean in any required direction for any purpose. The movements of body and limbs are all quite independent of each other (see Fig. 11 and 12).

It is by means of balance that we obtain and retain an independent seat. By maintaining balance and going with the horse, we do not need to grip the saddle tightly with our knees nor do we need to 'hang-on' with our hands.

Our seat, our security, should be quite independent of our limbs, and apart, from the grace and ease that go with balance, the horse is able to deal with our weight so much more easily.

30

Fig. 11

NEEDED IN ALL GOOD HORSEMANSHIP:

"AN INDEPENDENT SEAT is one that gives the utmost security and steadiness in the saddle while leaving the rider's limbs and weight of his body free . . . first to control the horse and then for any purpose he might have in mind . . ."

Mrs Kathy Bailey demonstrating an 'independent seat' in what is now becoming a most popular riding sport for both sexes — tent-pegging.

Fig. 12

. . . and Kathy scores a 'Carry'.

The Ladies' Tent-pegging Team won the Adelaide Equestrian Expo '80 Tent-pegging Championships. "Rishamra", a most versatile horse, began his education in dressage classes.

31

In a really good display of dressage, the horse will appear to read the rider's thoughts rather than obey his aids. Every effort is made by the rider to keep his aids invisible. Our aim is to get the maximum requirement from the horse with no apparent effort on the part of the rider.

The slightest change of balance or the tiniest movement of the rider's bodyweight can become an aid — a direction or signal. By preceding the necessary change of balance it makes the required movement easier for the horse: it not only warns the horse of the movement we are about to demand of him, but it facilitates the making of that movement. Later in the horse's education the weight of the rider's body will become a most important aid . . . probably the *most* important.

It is only after we have developed an independent seat that we can hope to improve on our control of the horse. Until we have developed it, there is no chance of us using our aids consistently. Complete control of ourselves must necessarily precede control of the horse we ride.

All the careful positioning of body and limbs are essential preliminaries to produce an 'INDEPENDENT SEAT'.

WHAT ARE THE AIDS?

SOME TERMS AND DEFINITIONS

The term 'aids' includes all the means by which we control the ridden horse — or should I say, 'the Dressage horse'? Some schools divide the aids used into 'Natural Aids' and 'Artificial Aids', and it might be useful to know what these terms mean.

Natural Aids includes the legs, hands, voice and the displacement of weight — the seat.

Artificial Aids take in what might well be called 'extensions of the natural aids' and include things such as whips, spurs, etc., all man-made items that more or less exaggerate or increase the effects of the 'natural aids'.

LATERAL AND DIAGONAL AIDS

We also occasionally hear someone refer to the aids as 'Diagonal Aids' or 'Lateral Aids'.

Lateral Aids: this term is used when the predominating aids are both on the same side of the horse; the left leg and the left hand constitute the left lateral aids, and the right leg and right hand constitute the right lateral aids.

Diagonal Aids: this term is used when the predominating aids are placed diagonally opposite each other; the left hand and right leg constitute the left diagonal aids, and the right hand and left leg constitute the right diagonal.

LATERAL AND DIAGONAL EFFECTS

In addition to lateral aids and diagonal aids, riders sometimes speak of lateral *effects* and diagonal *effects*.

By *'lateral effect'* is meant the aids used (whatever they might be) to move the whole horse to one side: both forehand and hindquarters are moved to the same side.

'Diagonal effect' means the aids used (whatever they might be) to move the forehand to one side and the hindquarters to the other.

It is important that we know and fully realise that they are anything but the same thing. Diagonal aids can produce lateral *effects* and lateral aids can produce diagonal *effects*.

Be sure you read what is said under the heading of 'Contact' [Ch. 5] *for lateral or diagonal aids do NOT mean that contact is lost with the other hand or leg. We maintain — or keep — contact with BOTH legs and BOTH hands.* These terms merely indicate that the aids nominated *PREDOMINATE.*

Chapters 19 and 20 are devoted to LATERAL MOVEMENTS.

☆   ☆   ☆

TO SUM UP

Before we can use our aids consistently we have to develop a seat that leaves our hands and legs free and independent.

Until we have developed an independent seat there is no chance of using our aids delicately and consistently.

Natural Aids — include the legs, hands, voice and displacement of weight [seat].

Artificial Aids — all man-made extensions of the natural aids: whips, spurs, etc.

Lateral Aids: predominating aids are both on the same side of the horse.

Diagonal Aids: predominating aids are diagonally opposite each other and take the name of whichever hand is used: left or right.

Lateral Effect: aids used to move both forehand and hindquarters to the same side.

Diagonal Effect: aids used to move forehand to one side and the quarters the other.

CHAPTER 5

CONTACT ...

REIN AND LEG
HORSE AND RIDER

Contact — and Ballroom Dancing;
Contact 'One'; Establishing Contact;
Changes of contact;
The expression 'Keep'.

CONTACT

Before I go further I feel I should first say something about the meaning of the term 'Contact'. It is important that we all understand what it means so that each clearly understands the other when we use it.

I have compared horse and rider with good dancing partners, in that they must first establish and then maintain a light contact, one with the other.

In highly skilled ballroom dancing, it is from this constant and light contact plus an alert and keenly developed sense of 'feel' that the lady is able to anticipate her partner's next movement and step with him as though they were one. This is the type of relationship we aim to establish between horse and rider.

An independent seat is necessary to give us the basic stability needed.

To maintain the most exact and maximum control of the horse in dressage, we have first to establish a contact with both our hands and with both our legs. A light and equal contact each side, legs and hands. The trained horse is held lightly between legs and hands: the legs creating impulsion and the hands controlling the energy created.

We should eventually be able to place our horse not only exactly where we want to place him but also have him step when and HOW we want — step long, short, high, fast, or slow, as we may require of him.

This is a very high ideal and although all do not attain to it we should know of it — and have it in mind when we begin with our own riding education and also with the education of each horse that comes into our hands.

The contact through the reins at the front should always
balance that of the legs at the back.

How light that contact will be will vary from one occasion to another. It will also vary with each different horse and each different rider. The horse has to learn — and we have to teach him — that when the rider increases the normal contact with either his legs or his hands, it means a demand is being made upon him. As the horse acts upon the order given, the rider returns to normal contact.

How — in the fewest words — can I get you to understand me when I want you to increase the weight or strength of your contact . . ? By how much . . ?

First, let me describe 'normal' contact.

Fig. 13
Riding in Contact: the rider sitting with his seat well forward in his saddle and his stirrup immediately under his weight; the line elbow to horse's mouth is straight — and note the attention of the horse. Photo courtesy Sister A. Komoraus [Vienna].

CONTACT 'ONE'

When instructing I refer to the normal strength — or lightness — of this *unknown and varying weight* on leg and hand as: 'Contact 1', or as just 'One'.

Although the normal weight (lightness) of the contact of leg or hand varies with each horse and each rider, I will refer to it, no matter how light or heavy it may be, as 'One'.

'One' or '1' then, is the term I use to indicate the normal weight of contact between each particular horse and his rider. The better the horseman and the better trained his horse, the lighter will be the contact and the lighter the aids.

35

Later, seat pressures or aids will take the place of even these so light leg aids (see Ch. 22 'Ultimate Aids').

CHANGES OF CONTACT

If at any time I want to ask a rider to increase *slightly* the weight of any contact, I need only say: 'Increase contact (hand or leg) to '1.1' — or it might be to '1.05'. This method is particularly useful when we want the rider to increase his light contact by only a very small fraction: we may even ask for an increase to only '1.01'.

Lightness in both hand and leg is most desirable and we work constantly at ourselves and our horse to improve his — and our own — lightness. Towards the end of his training we will be seeking a contact so light that changes in the aids will be so small as to be completely invisible to the onlooker.

Such extreme lightness, however, is not desirable in the early stages of training for on occasion the young horse might find it too difficult, too confusing. Just as a child learns his alphabet from large letters, we too should make our aids quite plain and clear at first.

ESTABLISHING CONTACT

Towards the latter part of the young horse's early schooling we gradually and progressively attempt to establish a very light contact with our legs and hands, and to get the horse to accept that as our normal relationship when we are not riding on a loose rein.

We are content at first if we can establish the contact without the youngster becoming in any way upset; but once he has learned to accept our contact of leg and hand we then start to think of getting him to play his part in the maintenance of that light contact. **In the earliest stages it is the rider who maintains the contact — but gradually our horse is brought to do his share in keeping the contact at '1'.**

Should our leg aids become stronger, be increased say to '1.1' and our rein contact remain at '1' then we are clearly asking the horse to increase his pace or impulsion to that degree.

It will be for us to show him, to teach him, that when he does so our leg contacts will return to '1'. HE LEARNS TO GO FORWARD TO MAINTAIN '1' — OR TO GET US TO RETURN TO '1' WITH OUR LEGS. (Ch. 7 has more to say about forward—driving aids).

Likewise should our hands increase their contact to say, '1.1' while the leg contact remains at '1', *the horse* has to correct the imbalance by reducing pace, whereupon it is for us to see that our hands return to **'One'** again.

Do notice that I have said nothing about reducing leg or hand contacts to less than '1' when any other aid is increased. On the contrary we have to be alert to see that none of our contacts ever drop below '1'.

> OUR AIM IS TO DEVELOP A PARTNERSHIP IN WHICH BETWEEN US — HORSE AND RIDER — WE ESTABLISH AND MAINTAIN A CONTACT OF "1".

This is the difference between 'contact' and a loose rein.

We increase our contact only when we ask or demand something of the horse, 'One' is normal, and we do not abandon it, but if we increase the weight of either leg or hand the horse has to learn — WE HAVE TO TEACH HIM — what he has to do to get us to return it to normal.

It is for us to see that our contact does not drop below '1' . . . and it is for our horse to see that we do not need to let it remain above '1'. The important difference is that the aids start from '1' — a normal light contact — not from a loose rein which is 'none'.

Fig. 14
Riding in contact: Miss Rachel Kalleske on her "Templewood Li'l Fluke" in an Encourage Test at the Dressage Club grounds, South Parklands, City of Adelaide.
An excellent performance. Rider's position very good, 'sitting down' and 'sitting up'.
Looking well up, she shows she can feel that her horse is doing what is wanted. Note the comfortable fit of the bridle and the line from elbow to bit.
Pony and rider look to be enjoying their test.

This is the ideal we keep in mind. From now on we will aim to be in contact with both legs and both hands, at least until WE decide to drop back to a loose rein — which we should repeatedly do.

And remember, when increasing the leg contact, always have your weight well down in the saddle.

CONTACT = BOTH HANDS AND BOTH LEGS

THE EXPRESSION 'KEEP'

We will often hear an instructor say something like: "Inside leg and outside rein". Just that; as if he had never heard of 'contact' as I have just described.

The instructor NEVER means *only* use one hand or one leg. He means that we should *increase the influence* of that particular leg or hand mentioned so that it has a more noticeable, stronger, or different effect than the other. He expects you, and often tells you, to KEEP the other hand or leg.

I would like you to particularly note the word, 'KEEP'.

Whenever it is used in these pages or by your instructor, you will find it to be used with deliberation — for no other word conveys quite so clearly and so concisely what the word 'keep' should convey.

To 'keep' a thing — anything — you must first HAVE that thing: you must first possess it or hold it.

The instructor is aiming to convey to you: "I assume you already have contact with the other leg (or rein); please KEEP — or maintain — that contact".

To 'keep' a leg or rein contact means: "Keep or maintain the contact you already have on that aid: DO NOT DROP OR LOOSEN THE CONTACT YOU ALREADY HAVE".

An independent seat and the ability to ride with 'contact' are absolutely essential to good horsemanship.

TO SUM UP

Horse and rider must first establish and then maintain a light contact, one with the other.

The trained horse is held lightly between leg and hand: the legs creating impulsion and the hands controlling the energy created.

'Contact 1' is the term I use to indicate the normal weight of contact between each particular horse and his rider.

This term is useful to enable the lightest changes in contact to be indicated, as from '1' to '1.01'.

The rider maintains contact in early stages of training, gradually teaching the horse to correct imbalanced aids for himself.

To maintain a contact is to 'keep' that contact.

CHAPTER 6

'ABOUT DRESSAGE'

Are you a 'thinking rider'?
A trained horse is the best instructor;
Dressage will help you.

ARE YOU A THINKING RIDER?

Almost every first class dressage rider I have seen demonstrate his art has been taught by a trained horse or horses as well as by a good instructor. Each horse used for this purpose has first to be brought up to the necessary standard of training. The trained rider is essential to the education of the horse to be used, and the trained horse is just as essential to the education of the successful rider.

Each horse and each rider teaches his partner by 'feel' and the response to 'feel'. *It is the condition of 'On the Bit' that is so elusive, so hard to explain — and so hard to understand from the written and spoken word. A trained horse is the best instructor . . . he teaches his rider to recognise the 'feel' of 'ON THE BIT'.*

In this book it is the rider we are most interested in. If he goes to a good riding school — and in the case of dressage that always includes a sufficient number of well-schooled horses — he is first taught to sit correctly (on the lunge usually) and given an independent seat, and in due course he is introduced to the aids *on a well-schooled horse.*

As he learns to use the aids (the controls) correctly, the pupil-rider produces in the trained horse he is riding the effect required by his instructor. When the pupil does the right thing, the trained horse responds in the right way too. It is easy for the pupil to learn the correct aids as the trained horse responds correctly *only* to the correct aids.

The horse clearly shows the rider when he is using correct aids — and just as clearly shows him when his aids are faulty. In this way the rider learns to use himself and the aids correctly and comes to recognise the feel of the correct responses — which will include the elusive condition of 'On the Bit'.

In the course of time and with practice, the pupil-rider comes to demand the correct responses from his horse and will accept nothing less. If he is riding a trained horse that is not working up to standard or is lazy, or perhaps inattentive, the rider also comes to recognise in what way the horse's behaviour falls short — and the appropriate action to take to correct it. First he learns to feel and recognise what is right, and eventually will not be happy when the horse responds other than correctly.

39

The young rider should never miss any opportunity to ride a well-trained horse.

WHY? ... AND WHY NOT?

I have also noticed that the trained horse teaches the young rider to accept the instructor's advice without question. The responses of the horse are proof of the effectiveness of the instruction. Usually the pupil is not encouraged to ask questions, and the instructor does not expect to have to explain the 'why' of what he is teaching.

Once I asked a first-class instructor from Europe: "What explanation would your instructor have given if you had asked him how those aids worked?" I was answered with a laugh and, "I once heard someone ask Otto Lorke something like that. His reply in crescendo, was: "Do it. DO IT. DO IT: and you'll find why you do it!"

Only too often the top exponents of the art of dressage can produce the effects aimed for, can teach their horses and then with the aid of the trained horse can teach others. But most of them do not attempt to explain 'how' and 'why' the effect is produced. They themselves learned without a lot of explanation: they learned to DO — not to talk. They were taught 'WHAT' to do; not 'WHY'.

A very good way to learn and if you have the time and the money to study in Europe — or in a first class school anywhere — I recommend you take their course. But to know 'WHY' often helps when difficulties present themselves (ask any cook!).

CAN I HELP EXPLAIN THE 'WHY' AND 'WHEREFORE' OF WHAT YOUR INSTRUCTOR TELLS YOU?

I hope I can: and in any case, in this book I'm going to 'give it a go'.

I have never trained any horse up to the highest levels of dressage, although I have taken a horse as far as the Medium and Advanced Medium stages. On the other hand I have repeatedly made dangerous horses into safe horses, disobedient horses into happy and co-operative horses, and have corrected times out of number bolters, jibbers, buckers — and scores of others with less common faults. I have used the principles of dressage for this purpose.

In each case, I start off to study the horse in question. I notice how he behaves, both in stables and out, when he is ridden and when he is not ridden. I do all I can to find out how the horse sees things: what makes him 'tick'. I study his character.

I first search for — and usually find — a reason or a possible reason, for the horse's behaviour. Then I look for a way of dealing with that problem, keeping in mind all I have noticed about his character. I find that to help the horse I must understand him and try to see his problem, whatever it might be, from HIS POINT OF VIEW.

I do not aim to write for the advanced and highly skilled dressage 'artist'. I write to help those who first need to know the steps that lead up past the level I have reached.

The late Mr Franz Mairinger told me it is considered to be a very great compliment to be described at the Spanish Riding School in Vienna as: 'a Thinking rider'.

Are you prepared to study dressage as well as practise it? Can you attend? Can you apply first your mind, and then whatever skill you may have?

... Can I start you thinking?

... If I can — then I will have done you a real service.

☆   ☆   ☆

DRESSAGE WILL HELP YOU

Any horseman will find dressage well worth any study he may care to give it for it is based on the soundest rules of horse education. A knowledge of even the first stages of dressage will be found helpful in the training of *any* horse for *any* purpose.

This does not mean that teaching a horse dressage will necessarily help in the schooling of racehorses, stock horses, polo ponies etc., but I do confidently assert that understanding the principles of dressage will help YOU, just as it has helped me.

When problems arise with any horse you may be training for whatever purpose you may be training him, the rules followed when training for dressage will be found to be most useful.

Learn how to teach (educate) a horse; learn the guiding principles. Learn the principles of dressage — and what lessons should precede others. The Tests are graded and so clearly tell us what we should start with — and what we should pass on to next.

And — if it is a racehorse you are training — see that all your horses go through the 'Go-Forward' Lesson (Ch. 10 'HORSE CONTROL — THE YOUNG HORSE'). Or . . . do you take it for granted, without thought, that it is 'natural' that if you hurt a horse's mouth he will go slower — but if you hurt him anywhere else he will go faster . . .?

TO SUM UP

A trained horse is the best instructor for any rider. He obeys when the rider uses the correct aids but he cannot obey when his rider uses what amounts to a language he cannot understand: the wrong aids.

When riding a trained horse, a rider need not know WHY this or that combination of aids is used; he only needs to know WHAT to do.

But to know 'WHY' as well as 'HOW' increases the rider's knowledge and understanding. To quote the late Mr Franz Mairinger: "To be considered a *thinking rider* is one of the greatest compliments of the Spanish School in Vienna".

The rules of dressage will help towards progressive training, simple lessons lead to more difficult ones, and their precepts have been proved over the centuries.

Even if a rider has no intention of practising dressage for its own sake, its progressive lessons will help with any horse that comes his way.

CHAPTER 7

LEG AIDS AND COMBINED AIDS

Leg aids must predominate — ALWAYS;
Meaning of the term 'Legs';
Increased leg contact should be intermittent;
Importance of Impulsion; Use and wearing of spurs;
Rein Effects;
Combining the Aids:
  In Early Training obedience to the leg imperative;
  The rein aids are more difficult to teach;
  Be tolerant when teaching rein aids.

LEG AIDS MUST PREDOMINATE — ALWAYS

Leg aids must predominate — always — and their use must always precede the rein aids even when riding into a halt or a rein-back (the latter part of this sentence will be fully explained later, in Ch. 11 'On the Bit').

Whenever I say 'leg' I will be referring to the calf of the leg — or to be more exact, to the inner side of the shin-bone at the level of the calf or a little lower; never to the muscle of the calf at the *back* of the leg.

In the earliest stages of training after breaking-in we may have to use the heel quite strongly on some horses to draw attention to, and to enforce obedience to, the leg. But whenever the word 'leg' is used in this work, it is meant to refer to *increased and intermittent* pressures of the legs at about the level of the calf.

Heels and whip, if and when used, should only enforce attention and obedience to the pressures applied at about calf height.

Normally we should use the legs at this height first; then if necessary we draw the young horse's attention to the legs, first by a light tap or two with the leg and then by the use of the heel. If we have to follow with a light tap with the whip, it should be more in the nature of a reminder than a disciplinary measure — with a young horse.

Remember, I am assuming you have thoroughly taught the 'Go-Forward' Lesson before mounting (see Ch. 10, 'HORSE CONTROL — THE YOUNG HORSE').

LEG PRESSURES SHOULD BE INTERMITTENT

To get the horse light to the leg we should never maintain a *constant* increased pressure when we require an increase of impulsion.

The increased contact or pressure of our legs should be intermittent — light and short and more in the nature of tiny taps or throbs than constant pressures or squeezes. The moment the horse responds to the legs, the legs must return to their normal steady light contact again.

OBEDIENCE TO THE LEG IMPERATIVE

Repeated use of the heels by a rider is *proof positive* that he has failed to get the horse to attend to lighter aids. Do not hesitate to revert to disciplinary measures when it is obviously necessary and you are *certain* that the horse understands — and is just 'loafing on you'.

Teach him what is wanted first and then insist on obedience.

When I am on a horse that is 'dead to the leg' I find myself thinking along the lines: "I'll give you such a biff in the bread-basket, my boy, if you don't take more notice of my legs . ."; and the implied threat in my thoughts often seems all that is necessary to wake him up. I find, too, that thinking in such off-hand terms tends to stop me losing my temper and perhaps becoming unnecessarily sharp. But . . . if he continues to loaf . . . I let him know in no uncertain manner that I am quite determined he has to be as nice to me as I am prepared to be towards him.

Your horse is useless for dressage and for most other purposes if he will not respond to the legs by increasing impulsion. We want to be nice to him and we take these progressive steps that draw his attention to our legs: we do this at first to give him every opportunity to avoid heels or whip. But we must also give him to understand that we have no intention of going on and on with this procession of reminders.

Later, we hope to be able to substitute seat (bone) pressures and changes of our balance for even our lightest leg aids — but how foolish to dream of an increase of impulsion in answer to a change of seat pressure if we cannot first get our horse to attend to the pressures of our legs.

Response to a light pulsing of the legs is a MUST. Until you can get this first simple requirement, you must face up to the fact that you have failed your grade and will not be ready to tackle the next until you prove successful with this.

Everything I have to say in any of my books presupposes an ability on your part to obtain from your horse, by slightly increased intermittent pressures of the legs, a corresponding surge forward. Without this all the rein effects fail.

> An increase of impulsion in obedience to the legs,
> corresponding in degree to the strength or lightness
> of the pressures, is an absolute prior necessity.

IMPORTANCE OF IMPULSION

You can do little with any kind of transport until you can get it to move forward. You first have to be able to create forward impulsion, even though later on you may want some degree of sideways movement.

In this matter we might compare a ridden horse with a sailing boat — even when the breeze is in the wrong direction, to the north say, you can change a boat's direction to the east or west. But without the wind — the drive, the impulsion — the sailors have no control and the boat can only drift.

The same with our horse.

The importance of response to the leg is not limited to dressage: no matter what the horse is wanted for he will be useless if you cannot get him to go forward when required — whether he wants to or not. Without forward response to the legs a horse is as little use as a bicycle without a chain.

IN THE EARLY LESSONS WE TEACH OUR HORSE THE LEGS MEAN — AND ONLY MEAN — 'GO FORWARD'; AND HE MUST GO FORWARD IN ANSWER TO LIGHT LEG AIDS. NOT UNTIL LATER WILL WE ADD A LATERAL EFFECT OF A DRAWN-BACK LEG.

Until the rider feels for and insists on obedience to the forward drive of the legs neither he nor his horse can possibly attain to even the lower levels of dressage.

SPURS

You may notice I have not mentioned the use of spurs in these early lessons. Even later in his schooling, I recommend you revert to an appropriate tap with the whip if he fails to respond to the legs. When later again, you do use spurs, be sure you introduce them to the horse gently and progressively — as with everything new.

Do not use spikes or rowels in the spurs if you can possibly avoid it when first using them; you can always wrap something around the rowels should you not have another pair.

Do not turn your toes out when you first use spurs. Use the inside edge of the spur and the inside of the neck of the spur: and introduce them progressively. A lot of horses resent them at first.

Until horse and rider reach the higher levels of dressage, rowels will do more harm than good and they should not be necessary in early training. When used in more advanced dressage, the rowels should just lie in the hair of the horse's coat and the horse respond to the lightest possible change of contact.

... IN PASSING ... BOOTS AND SPURS

Have you ever noticed how high is the blocked-out section of the heels of good riding boots? This high blocking is not found in any other boot and is built-in

45

to provide a seat or base for spurs to sit, quite high up, (see Fig. 15). (In days now past, Weedon Cavalry School in England required students to wear their spurs ABOVE the ankle.)

You will also have noticed that almost all spurs have upward bent necks. The higher the spur, the easier it is to contact the horse *and the more delicately we can use them.* The lower the spur the more difficult it is to lightly contact the horse — due to the curving of his body.

Fig. 15
Sketch of a good type of riding boot. The high blocking-out of the heel gives a firm base for a spur to be adjusted to any height. The high blocking of the heel also makes it almost impossible for the rider's foot to be trapped in a stirrup iron (see Ch. 26).
The inner side of the top of the boot should be a little lower than the outer side.

REIN EFFECTS

I have dealt fully with rein effects in Chapter 18 of 'HORSE CONTROL — THE YOUNG HORSE'. All sports and professions have terms or names that lend themselves to brevity and exactness during instruction and conversation: do **you** know what is meant by the terms:

1 . . . an 'open rein'?
2 . . . a 'direct rein'?
3 . . . a 'neck rein'?
4 . . . an 'indirect rein'?
5 . . . an 'indirect rein of opposition'?

Many riders not only do not know of these names, but they are also unaware of the reins having the effects described. I will assume my reader to be familiar with that Chapter.

COMBINING THE AIDS

RESPONSE TO LEG AIDS IN EARLY TRAINING

During his earliest stages of training, the horse will have been taught that when we use both legs we want him to understand them to mean: 'Move forward' or 'Move faster' or perhaps, 'Don't Stop'.

Later on we include lateral effects — but throughout the early lessons the legs mean and should ONLY mean: 'Go forward to the degree indicated by the strength or lightness of the rider's leg pressures'.

On no account should we complicate these first simple Go-forward lessons by trying to introduce any sideways responses to our legs.

The drawn-back leg when we do start to use it, will mean: 'Move your quarters away from this pressure AND GO ON'.

And if the pressure of the drawn-back leg is greater, or stronger, than before its position was changed, its additional pressure also includes: 'Continue to go on and forward — move with *increased* impulsion'.

> NO LATERAL DEMAND OF EITHER ONE LEG IS EVER ALLOWED TO INTERFERE WITH OR DIMINISH THE FORWARD DRIVE OF **BOTH** LEGS.

THE REIN AIDS ARE MORE DIFFICULT TO TEACH

It would simplify schooling if we could do with our reins as we can with our legs: teach only the 'slow down' or 'stop' effect of the reins at first and only much later introduce the second and additional effect, a turning effect. But this we cannot do.

Just as an additional pressure on either one leg should increase the forward drive of both legs, so too should additional weight on either one rein increase the stopping effect of both reins.

This is a complication with the reins that adds to the young horse's difficulties (and ours) as we have to use both these rein effects from the first day our horse is ridden. It is for this reason that we use an open rein at first . . . an 'open rein', you will remember, has little or no stopping effect.

COMBINING THE AIDS

As his training progresses, the young horse comes to recognise that although a tightening of one rein means 'check pace and turn this way', the use of the rider's legs at the same time is meant to counter its stopping effect.

> HE HAS TO BEGIN TO WEIGH THE EFFECTS OF ONE AID AGAINST THE OTHER, AND THIS WEIGHING OF ONE AID AGAINST THE OTHER BECOMES MORE AND MORE IMPORTANT AS TRAINING GOES ON.

It is the first step towards 'combined aids', and one we would avoid in these early stages if we could.

BE TOLERANT WHEN TEACHING REIN EFFECTS

It is essential that the trainer recognises the *difficulties that face the horse* when we are teaching him what the reins have to mean. From the first day he is ridden the reins must necessarily have these two meanings: we must be tolerant and realise that becoming heavier with our hands and hurting his mouth will not help the horse to understand. It will only spoil his mouth and upset him. Progress with the reins will be slower and we must in no way try to hurry.

The bit can hurt the horse so much that he loses his calmness: and calmness is essential to easy and quick learning.

There is a decided advantage in teaching as much as possible of these essential aids well before the horse is mounted (see the 'Go-forward Lesson', 'Driving from Over the Saddle', and 'Yielding to a Stretched Rein' in 'HORSE CONTROL — THE YOUNG HORSE'. These lessons not only make things so much easier for the young horse but they help to give him a light mouth).

Early training is simplified for the horse if the trainer teaches the simplest aids first — before the horse is mounted.

TO SUM UP

'Legs' refers to the use of the legs at calf-height. Use of the rider's heels should only follow when the horse fails to answer the leg pressures.

Increase of leg pressures should be by light, short pressures more like taps or vibrations than squeezes. The legs should return to their normal contacts as the horse responds by increased impulsion.

Be very tolerant at first. As with all lessons, we must be sure that the horse understands what the legs are intended to mean *before* we become sharper with him. He should have been taught the "Go-forward" lesson before he was first mounted.

A horse that will not increase impulsion in answer to our leg aids is as useless as a sailing ship without a wind. You can neither start nor turn.

Spurs should not be used in early schooling. When and if used later, they should be fitted very high on the riding boot. The horse must be brought to answer the *legs*.

We FIRST teach the horse that our legs mean — and ONLY mean — "Go Forward"; and that the strength or lightness with which we use our legs indicates the degree of impulsion required.

To avoid confusing the horse we do not, in early schooling, attempt to include any lateral effect from our legs. That comes later in his training.

The rein aids, on the other hand, hold two meanings from the very beginning of his training: a stopping effect and also a turning effect.

There is no way in which we can avoid this double meaning of the reins. It complicates matters for the horse and probably explains why responses to light rein aids are usually more difficult to obtain than light responses to the legs.

The horse has to learn to weigh the reins against the legs — and this is the beginning of what is known as "Combined Aids".

CHAPTER 8

'TASTING THE BIT'

Tasting the bit is a sign of relaxation;
A natural occurence;
A step towards flexion;
Nervousness, tension or resistance.

TASTING THE BIT

The term 'tasting the bit' refers to a small movement of the horse's tongue and his bottom jaw as he is being ridden forward or is at the halt. To an onlooker it might appear that the bit could have a nice taste. As this 'tasting' seldom occurs except when he is content and relaxed, the horse might well be thinking: 'The world's all right!' He is happy, relaxed and co-operative — and is showing it.

To taste the bit, the horse does not necessarily open his mouth, and when he does do, as he occasionally will, it should be only for a moment or so. He moves his tongue and bottom jaw for a moment or two — and this he may do several times. — much like a cook tasting a sauce or gravy . . . not chewing, but 'tasting'.

The horse is also finding that he can, while still keeping contact, slightly lighten the feel of the bit by just moving his tongue and jaw — and most important to him, that his doing so *pleases his rider.*

His lightening the bit allows his rider to lighten leg contacts a fraction, so that horse and rider can ride on with lighter contact all round . . . legs and hands.

At first the horse does not taste the bit to please the rider; he probably will not even notice when he is doing it, although his doing so lightens the feel on the bit. But we want to make use of this sign of relaxation and be able to induce the horse to 'taste the bit' to our command — which amounts to *relaxing to our command.*

If we have been riding 'in contact' for some weeks, we should expect the horse to show us by this tasting that he is contented, relaxed and ready for a lighter contact — a very satisfactory relationship between horse and rider.

As the rider wants to encourage the horse to taste the bit, he does so by praising and rewarding the horse the moment it occurs. After a number of repetitions the horse will come to realise that it is his relaxing and 'tasting the bit' that pleases his rider.

"FEEL" THE HORSE TASTE THE BIT

The rider, on his part, has first to learn to recognise the feel of his horse tasting the bit. We should learn to feel for this action as we should feel for everything else the horse does: 'Look UP: Stretch UP: Sit DOWN; **Feel DOWN**'.

This is an important part of the horse's training. Don't hurry. Take time, and be ready to encourage him the *moment* you feel his slightest tendancy to taste the bit as you ride on.

We should not try to keep the horse tasting the bit; our aim at this early stage is to get him to relax readily and often rather than for long periods. First we try to get him to realise that we want. Later we will, as usual, ask for more.

ENCOURAGE INSTANTLY

As with all lessons, rewards and encouragements should be instant. Before we begin we should have our minds made up as to when and how we will encourage our horse. We should be *waiting for the opportunity* to be able to convey to him: 'That's it! You clever horse . . .", by rein and voice — as well as immediately lightening our leg contacts a fraction.

Why lighten the leg contacts? . . . Because he has just lightened the rein contact a tiny fraction (see Ch. 5 'Contact'). The rider should repeatedly check that he, too, is relaxed: 'Down the Weight'.

A NATURAL OCCURRENCE

A demonstration film of Mr Maurice Wright using the Jeffery Method of breaking-in an untouched wild station brumby was taken by my wife Pat a little time ago. In the film it is most noticeable that as the wild horse comes to realise he has little reason to fear his handler, he becomes more and more relaxed — and shows it by lightly moving his tongue and jaw as if 'smacking his lips'. This smacking of the lips also tells the handler he is working on the right lines.

The following report in our local paper, 'The Advertiser', is interesting too, as it shows that this movement of the tongue and mouth is not confined to horses. I quote:

> "She [the psychologist] plays it to them and watches their response. Played loudly it wakes a new-born child, who stretchs and smacks its lips with pleasure. It positively basks in the pleasure of the long familiar sound."

The paragraph refers to the reproduction of pre-natal sounds or rhythms — and in each of these cases the smacking of the lips is a sign of relaxation.

51

[F.E.I. Rule 402 sets out the requirements of the 'Halt' and it is interesting to note that the rule includes — 'The horse may *quietly champ the bit* while maintaining a light contact with the rider's hands.']

A STEP TOWARDS FLEXIONS

Tasting the bit will lead towards flexions if we do not hurry. Flexing is a little more than repeated and sustained 'tasting' when driven forward by the legs.

Remember, if the horse goes up to the bit — if he goes forward in answer to the legs and keeps the reins light — the whole horse, right up to his ears, will go forward a tiny fraction. He has to learn to taste the bit and to flex so that he can go slightly forward — and up to the bit — as demanded by the legs.

We have him started on the way to collection and 'on the bit'.

THE HORSE THAT 'POKES HIS NOSE'

When the horse moves with his head too high and his nose out, we should never try to get him to lower it by pulling on the reins. The fact is that under these conditions the horse is stiff: the very opposite of being relaxed.

We cannot FORCE a horse to relax — for horses resist force.

If we can get him to relax, the horse will gradually lower his head and the rider should just maintain a light contact with the mouth. We have to encourage him to relax and allow his head to drop — and then later on start to feel for and to encourage him to taste the bit. Tasting the bit means he is relaxing; we cannot force a horse to relax.

NERVOUSNESS, TENSION OR RESISTANCE

'Tasting the bit' should never be confused with grinding the teeth or chewing.

Article 416 of the F.E.I. Rules includes: "Putting out the tongue, keeping it above the bit or drawing it up altogether, as well as grinding the teeth and swishing the tail are mostly signs of nervousness, tenseness or resistance on the part of the horse and must be taken into account by the judges in their marks for the movement concerned as well as in the collective mark for submission".

'Tasting the bit' is the answer to all this.

TO SUM UP

'Tasting the bit' defined as a small movement of the horse's tongue and jaw when he is being ridden forward — or at the halt — in contact.

Tasting the bit has the effect of lightening and mobilising the mouth contact with the bit; it is proof of the horse being calm and relaxed.

At first the horse does not taste the bit deliberately; it is just a sign of his being in a relaxed state.

To be able to induce the horse to taste the bit is the start of getting the horse 'to go up to the bit' when the legs demand 'forward'.

One cannot but notice that photographs of high grade dressage horses almost always show the horse with a light froth at the mouth due to his consistent tasting of the bit.

CHAPTER 9

CONTROL OF THE HEAD AND NECK

Teaching the horse to 'take rein';
'Showing the horse the way to the ground';
A 'springy' hand; A resistant hand;
'Taking rein' is part of early schooling;
The excitable horse;
'Taking' with one rein;
The Free Walk.

When we speak of 'Control of the Head and Neck' most riders think we have in mind to raise the horse's head and arch his neck.

We do keep that in mind but for much *later* in his schooling.

> WHAT IS SO MUCH MORE IMPORTANT IN THE HORSE'S EARLY SCHOOLING IS FOR THE RIDER TO BE ABLE TO INDUCE HIM TO LOWER HIS HEAD AND STRETCH OUT HIS NECK TO OUR DEMAND SO THAT WE CAN GET HIM TO STEP OUT WITH FULL EASY STRIDES.

We need to teach him first to answer our legs and then to **'take rein'**, particularly at the walk, the 'Free Walk'.

TEACHING THE HORSE TO 'TAKE REIN'

The length and position of the horse's neck affects the length of his stride, the height to which he lifts his feet, his speed — and also his balance.

A well-collected horse moves with his head held high and he also moves with short high steps. The higher the head is carried, the higher the muscles of the neck will draw the point of the shoulder and lift the foot. More important, this also shortens the length of the stride.

What is not so well known is that horses bred for racing tend to 'daisy-cut': an expression used to describe the stride of horses with low action — with the foot moving close to the ground. 'Daisy-cutters' stride long and low, and this makes for speed as no time or energy is lost lifting the foot unnecessarily high.

BALANCE

The position of his head has much to do with a horse's balance, too. A shorter neck and higher head carriage takes weight off the forelegs and tends to displace the weight more to the rear — and the horse becomes better balanced. A well-balanced horse carries the weight of both himself and his rider more equally divided between forehand and hindquarters. This, too, we will find has its advantages at times.

For the complete control of the horse then, it becomes quite clear that control of the head and neck is essential. Moreover, experience shows that in schooling, a long easy-moving stride must take precedence over anything in the nature of collection. Usefulness must take precedence over showiness — particularly in these early stages.

'SHOWING THE HORSE THE WAY TO THE GROUND'

Time after time during our horse's early schooling we will find it most useful to be able to induce him to stretch his neck forward and down. This applies particularly to any horse that becomes excited when ridden in company. On endless occasions we will want to convey to such a horse: 'Walk on, with long easy strides. Relax . . . lower and lengthen your neck so that you can lengthen your stride'.

This is what is known in some schools of equitation as 'Showing the horse the way to the ground'.

First we should learn about it and recognise its great usefulness — and then we should make a point of teaching it to every horse that passes through our hands. Time after time it will prevent the formation of difficult habits: and I need hardly remind you that 'Prevention is both better . . . and easier . . . than cure'.

How often the late Capt. J. J. Pearce said to me when I was riding a young horse at a walk: "I want his head down there, Tom, down there . .", pointing to the ground. As with all lessons it should be taught BEFORE it is needed and while the horse is calm and receptive. Establish the understanding as early as you can and keep in mind that *the horse must be calm to learn any lesson.*

THE HORSE SHOULD BE TAUGHT TO 'TAKE'
TO A YIELDING HAND

The horse's education consists of a number of steps or grades and many of the means we use early in his training are discarded after they have served their turn. The manner in which a child learns to spell out his first few words is quite different from the way he is expected to spell later on. His laborious reading of letter by letter gives way eventually to instant comprehension of a word of many syllables at one glance.

The same with our horse. The simpler we make his lessons at first, the easier he will grasp what is wanted and so the quicker we can progress to the next lesson. This applies to all lessons. I would like to show that this is so in this matter of 'taking rein'.

A 'SPRINGY' HAND

In teaching the horse to take rein we first use our legs to ask for some slight lengthening of the stride. To lengthen the stride he will usually need some slight lengthening of the neck. It is for us to see that our hands do all they can (short of going into loose rein) to encourage him to stretch his neck a little, by teaching him to 'take rein'.

To do this we have to see that our hands maintain a light springy contact with the horse's mouth: a contact devoid of either additional weight or resistance — a springy, spring-like contact (see Ch. 5 'Contact').

The word 'springy' although universally used, is not a particularly apt term; 'inviting' is probably a better definition.

What I want you to understand by 'springy' (or inviting) is for the rider's hand to produce a 'feel' on the horse's mouth such as would be produced by a light rein, if, instead of being held in the hand it passed over a small pulley held there. At the end of the rein on the other side of the imaginary pulley is attached a light weight, say an ounce — 30gr. — (or much less) or in any case a weight about equal to our usual 'contact 1' feel.

Should the horse stretch his head forward as we want him to, the weight on his mouth becomes no greater. Should he bring his head back, the weight becomes no less.

The horse soon comes to recognise that when the rein has this type of 'feel' on it — and as long as the same springy and inviting light feel is maintained — no stretching of head and neck will affect the feel or weight on his mouth. Such a 'feel' on the reins, when he understands it, will encourage him to act with confidence on the demand of the legs and stride freely on.

It is this sort of feel I have in mind when I speak of a 'springy' or inviting hand.

The horse soon recognises that the rider's springy hand means he is at liberty to move on and stretch his head and neck *for as long as the rider's hands remain light and 'inviting'.*

> When this 'feel' is linked with the drive of the legs it becomes an order to lengthen his stride and if he finds it helpful — to lengthen his neck too.

'TAKING' WITH ONE REIN — AND THE HORSE WITH A ONE-SIDED MOUTH

We will also find it necessary to teach our horse to take with a single rein as well as with both. For instance, being able to induce him to 'take' with the right

56

rein only, will bend his head and neck to the left — and his stretching or 'taking' with the left rein will bend him to the right [see Fig. 16].

Fig. 16
The horse 'takes' with one rein — top ranking Australian polo-player, Sinclair Hill.
Photo by courtesy of Sinclair Hill and 'The Equestrian'.

This is not only most useful in the early days when riding on curved lines but it leads to the secret of how to deal with a horse with a one-sided mouth. Such horses learn to straighten up much more easily when they are taught to take with the rein on the side to which they normally bend. They will learn to 'take' with that rein much more readily than to give (or yield) to the other rein.

Being able to ask our horse to stretch one rein, and in doing so his whole side, is particularly useful in more advanced work. First in the shoulder-in where the outside rein has to be kept stretched by the horse, and later again in more advanced movements.

As training progresses, 'taking' with the outside rein becomes more and more important as a means of bending the horse's head and neck, and to a lesser degree his spine.

How often do instructors urge: "Inside leg and outside rein", and follow that with: "KEEP the outside rein". We ask our horse to 'take' the outside rein — and it is then for *the rider* to keep that contact.

'Inside leg . . . outside rein': 'keep' that inviting springy outside rein — and above all things RIDE THE HORSE FORWARD.

Our horse has also to be taught that he may continue to take rein only to the point we have in mind. We may only want him to take rein for perhaps an inch (3 cm). At the end of that distance, or any other we may have in mind, he will feel the hands start to become resistant and we have to teach him that he has reached the limit asked of him.

A RESISTANT HAND

I have said a good deal about a resistant hand in 'HORSE CONTROL — THE YOUNG HORSE', but in case you do not have a copy handy, this summary will perhaps be helpful.

The use of side-reins when mouthing a horse before he has been ridden introduces the young horse to a resistant hand or rein. They show him that pushing against the reins once they are stretched and resistant, hurts his mouth. He learns in a very short time that the harder he pushes the more the bit hurts his mouth — but the moment he stops pushing against the reins, the pain ceases.

The girth to which the side-reins are fastened does not pull; it stays still. It just resists. It neither pulls nor gives.

This is what a resistant hand does: it keeps still when the horse applies force to it and remains still when he stops using force.

'Resistance MUST be equal to but CAN NEVER EXCEED the force it opposes.

Think it over.

A resistant hand does not move; it neither gives nor takes. It keeps still. But you need to be quite a good rider to keep your hand still: so that the rein *automatically* becomes lighter when the horse stops 'taking'. [The arm muscles used to maintain resistance are the same muscles as those used for putting a light tension on the reins — or pulling.)

'TAKING REIN' IS PART OF EARLY SCHOOLING

It is clear then, that teaching the horse to take rein is part of his early schooling and should be taught months before we even think of 'collection'.

Even in the show-ring, most knowledgeable judges want to see a hack stride on and cover ground effortlessly and lightly when asked to do so, as well as to move with a more collected and 'showy' carriage when required.

It is essential that we can 'turn on' an extended stride . . . and also 'turn it off' when desired.

Many of the bad habits that result from the horse becoming excited and fretting against a bit action he cannot understand, can be avoided by teaching him

58

to 'take rein' and lengthen his neck on demand.

Keep in mind that your horse will not have the faintest idea of what your 'springy' hand means when first you begin to use that condition. *Above all things, we must be most tolerant when he tries something other that what we have in mind.* When he tries to do other than what we want of him when we begin to teach him this or any other lesson, on no account should we punish him. We must assume that he is trying to find out what we want him to do.

We should quietly and gently persist with our aids until we feel him try, or even tend to try, something like that which we want of him. Then we have to convey to him: "**That's** better", or "**That** will profit you"; and we should immediately discontinue whatever aids we are using: 'End of Lesson'.

When our young horse tries the wrong thing we should convey to him: "Not that, dear; what you have just tried won't make me stop using these aids: that won't profit you. Try again." That "dear" I recommend you to use in your thinking is not 'sissy'; it helps to keep YOU calm and in a good temper.

THE EXCITABLE HORSE

You may have a horse with too much impulsion: one that always wants 'to go for his life' once he leaves his home ground. A horse that does not appear to know that you want him to go slower or at varying paces.

If, when you take your horse hacking, you find you cannot get him first to walk 'steady and relaxed' and then to quietly stride on with long relaxed strides at the easy pace of the walk — you will have very little chance of getting him to do so at the faster paces, as when in the hunting field or under other exciting conditions.

I recommend you first teach your horse to take rein, as just explained, at home; and when you think he is ready, take him out for short hacks. When you have him changing pace at the walk, striding on with longer — or shorter — steps, start doing the same thing at the trot, which you may find more difficult.

The first hacking rides with this sort of horse should be very short. If he becomes upset, go back to your home ground and there settle him down again. Be sure to make a big fuss of him the instant he takes rein and drops into a walk, at home or wherever he might be. Practise changes of pace again at home and let him see how pleased you are THE INSTANT he tends to calm down and lengthen his stride in answer to your legs — particularly if he tastes the bit. Nothing upsets a horse more than not being able to understand his rider.

It is for the rider to encourage every TENDANCY his horse shows of doing what is wanted. Anything in the way of punishment will upset an excitable horse. Let me again repeat what the late Mr Franz Mairinger so often said: "If the horse is not doing what you want, it will be because he does not understand you".

Most horses learn to take rein and move on at a free walk without difficulty; others accept it under calm circumstances but fail to lower and stretch their head and neck under more exciting conditions. It is for this reason I advise: "Teach the 'take rein' lesson to every horse that comes into your hands".

THE 'FREE WALK'

The walk is known as 'The Mother of the paces', and one of the earliest variations of pace asked for in dressage tests of the present day is 'The Free Walk' (see Ch. 14).

Now I will quote what the rules have to say about 'The Free Walk':

> "The Free Walk is a pace of relaxation in which the horse is allowed complete freedom to lower and stretch out his head and neck."

Fig. 17
THE FREE WALK is part of early schooling.
Miss Michelle Luscombe on 'Templewood-in-Vogue' demonstrates a 'Free Walk' in an Encourage Test at the Dressage Club Grounds. The pony steps out and lengthens his stride and the rider remains in contact.

The rule does not make it clear that the reins should be kept lightly stretched, with the horse 'taking rein'. As a result some riders mistake the term to mean 'a loose rein'. In all the several different tests I have here before me, a 'Free Walk on a long rein' is substituted for just a 'Free Walk'. This is a good practice as it makes quite clear to riders — and judges — that the reins should maintain a light 'inviting' contact (see Fig. 17).

At the Free Walk the horse is allowed this complete freedom to stretch out his head and neck. Contact with the mouth should be maintained when a free walk is asked for — but from it we should be able to drop the reins at any moment and continue on with a loose rein.

When schooling a young horse, a free walk on a loose rein should be used repeatedly, particularly when we want to reward our horse after he has done something well: 'End of Lesson' . . . 'That will profit you' . . . and all that.

I should stress, however, that even when on a completely loose rein, our horse has to maintain both the direction and the pace he was working at when the rider dropped his reins.

'THE PLOT FAILS . . .'

Some years ago, when I was riding the late Dorothy Mansom-Gray's thoroughbred 'Why Argue', (Fig. 18) I took him through the ususal 'take rein' lessons and soon had him going well at home. On longer trips or in strange surroundings however, he would 'bomb-up' and I found I could not get him to settle down by this method.

Fig. 18
The author at 73 on Mrs D. Mansom-Gray's "Why Argue". The knee-pads and bandages show we were still not sure at this stage that "Why Argue" would behave.

I found the following effective. If he continued to show no signs of relaxing and lowering his tightly-arched neck, we would prance along for perhaps a half-mile or so until we came to a piece of suitable ground — and then, instead of continuing to try to get him to relax by the 'take rein' method, I would change to

61

a very 'open rein' and completely loosen the other rein (see Ch. 18, 'HORSE CONTROL — THE YOUNG HORSE' — Open Rein). I showed him: "I am not going to worry you any more to lower your head and relax. You can go your hardest: *but on a very small circle*".

Using only the completely 'open rein' which has no stopping effect, I would put him on a circle of some two to three metres. This caused his hindquarters to fly out on a larger circle than the forehand — and soon steadied him down into a walk.

"That will profit you", I would instantly show him and I would continue on with the walk as his reward. I had to repeat the maneouvre several times before he realised what was wanted of him and I could easily imagine him thinking to himself: "Oh not again!", as I would revert to the open rein and circle on one or two later occasions. I have never had to revert to this measure with a young horse that had not raced.

TO SUM UP

It is most important that in the horse's early education he can be induced to lower his head and stretch out his neck.

A long easy-moving stride must take precedence over anything in the nature of collection. Learning to take rein is not a difficult lesson for the horse and should be mastered before any degree of collection is even thought of.

While he is calm, the horse is 'invited' to stretch his head and neck when the rider's legs increase their pressure and the hands become 'springy'. This is sometimes called: 'showing the horse the way to the ground".

It is most important that we can ask for and obtain a long and extended stride — at any pace — when desired.

Teaching the horse to 'take' with one rein will help in later schooling and is of *utmost importance* in advanced movements.

Having taught him to 'take rein' in manege or arena, we should take our horse for short walks outside his home ground. If he becomes upset, take him back home and repeat the 'take rein' lessons.

At a Free Walk the horse is allowed complete freedom to lower and stretch out his head and neck but the reins should maintain contact.

A Free Walk is asked for in the very earliest dressage tests and should be one of our first goals.

CHAPTER 10

THE HORSE SHOULD BE BENT IN THE DIRECTION
OF MOVEMENT ... WHY?

F.E.I. Rule 401;
Some mechanics of the horse's movement;
Lateral effects of the legs;
Aids to bend the horse's spine;
The 'inside' leg;
The 'outside' leg;
Importance of the 'inside' leg.

F.E.I. RULES

Rule No. 401 of the 1979 International Rules for Dressage includes: "The horse . . . remaining absolutely straight in any movement on a straight line and bending accordingly when moving on curved lines."

Rule No. 409 [1] states: "At changes of direction, the horse should adjust the bend of his body to the curvature of the line he follows, remaining supple and following the indications of the rider, without any resistance or change of pace, rhythm or speed."

The next paragraph continues: [2] "When changing direction at right angles, *for instance when riding corners*, the horse should describe one quarter of a circle of approximately 6 metres diameter at collected and working paces, and at medium and extended paces one-quarter of a circle of approximately 10 metres diameter" [see also Ch. 12 'Riding a Corner'].

Most horses have great difficulty in putting a pronounced bend in their spines when first under a rider. This explains why all circles asked for in early dressage tests are as large as the arena will allow — at least 20 metres in diameter. As the standard of the tests goes up the size of the circles required of the horse becomes smaller — and so the bend required on the horse's spine becomes correspondingly greater [see Fig. 19].

In each more advanced test the size of the circles asked for becomes progressively smaller until they reach the minimum size of 6 metres. [At that size they are called "voltes".]

The question I would expect a reader to be asking when reading the above is: "Why SHOULD the horse be bent in the direction of movement? The International Rules require it — but why?"

63

WHY SHOULD THE HORSE'S BODY BE BENT "ACCORDINGLY" WHEN MOVING ON CURVED LINES?

SOME MECHANICS OF HORSE MOVEMENT

Length, strength, height and ease of stride. The horse's limbs are controlled by muscles that like all muscles are able to contract and so shorten their length. The limb muscles are attached to a bone by tendons which act like a rope conveying the pull of the muscle to the bone.

Several things can influence the ease, freedom, extent and direction of the limb's movement. For instance, it is clear that the further a muscle is stretched *before* it is contracted the further it can move the limb when contraction occurs. As most of the muscles that draw the shoulder forward lie in the horse's neck, the more forward his neck is stretched the further forward those muscles can pull the shoulder as the horse moves.

Fig. 19
RIDING A CIRCLE   *Photograph by courtesy of Mrs John Rymill.*
Mr Andrew Rymill on "Reminiscent" at the Royal Windsor Horse Show, England.
*   We note the fully engaged off-hind leg as "Rem" circles and the even bend on his spine from ears to croup so that each leg moves to its front — forward — on different segments of the same circle.*
*   Horse and rider look in the direction of movement, with the rider's head well up. The rider sits 'deep', and both horse and rider are completely relaxed.*
*   Andrew's home was originally at "Old Penola", Penola, South Australia, but he has spent many years at his headquarters in England, 'Gracious Pond Stables', Chobham, Surrey.*

Conversely, as mentioned earlier, the higher the head is carried and so the shorter and higher the horse's neck, the higher his foot will be lifted and the shorter will be the stride.

For maximum efficiency the muscles that draw each pair of legs forward should always lie in the direction in which we want the legs to be drawn: to the front when the horse is moving on a straight line and *towards the direction of movement when he is moving on a curved line*. So positioned he can move forward with greater ease and with less effort, among other things.

We therefore find that Rule 401 aims at getting maximum efficiency from the horse's legs.

BODY-BENDING EFFECTS

THE 'TAKE REIN' LESSON

Just as the front and back wheels of a motor-car face in slightly different directions when following a bend, so too the front legs of the horse have to be drawn in a slightly different direction from the hind-legs when on a circle or part-circle. With a car, the stub-axle permits of this, and the horse's spine takes on that role for the horse.

As we have to ask our horse for changes of direction from the very earliest days of his training, it will be found to be an advantage to be able to bend him quite early.

If we have taught him to 'take rein' in his early schooling as we should have done [see Ch. 9], we can begin to bend his head and shoulders even before he learns the lateral meaning of the legs. We can start to do this at this stage of his training by asking him to 'take' with the outside rein. His doing so will stretch that side of his body and not interfere with or constrain his movement — his strides.

BODY-BENDING LEG AIDS: THE OUTSIDE LEG

So far we should have been most careful to teach our horse that our legs mean one thing, and one thing only — to move forward.

It is only after he has shown that he clearly understands this first essential that we think of adding a lateral — sideways — effect to our leg aids. But first I have to be sure my reader knows what aids to use to produce body-bending effects.

When riding forward on a straight line, the rider's legs should remain in the position as set out in Ch. 3, and we will find that this will place each leg very close to the rear edge of the girth. So placed — opposite each other and on or very close to the girth — any lateral effect they each hold will be countered by the leg on the opposite side of the horse. Both legs when used in this position should only drive the horse forward.

But . . . when we draw one leg back, each leg will be required to produce its own lateral effect in a different place *while still maintaining its forward drive.*

The drawn-back leg should TEND to push the horse's hindquarters away from itself — while the other leg, still at the girth, should TEND to push the forelegs towards ITS opposite side.

When we use a drawn-back leg we should normally draw it back only a few inches: the knee or thigh should not be drawn back. Our leg in this position is meant to affect the hindquarters and hind legs which lie about a metre behind the girth. The heel should stay down and the rider's seat-bones remain firm on the saddle.

Although when riding a trained horse the rider's outside leg should be drawn back no more than a hand's breadth at the very most, we might well draw it back a little further during the first stages of these early body-bending lessons. Our doing so will tend to draw the young horse's attention to its changed position — but this additional drawing back of the leg is not necessary and should not continue beyond the first few days.

Let us imagine we are going to ask our horse to bend his hindquarters to the LEFT on this occasion.

The rider's drawn-back right leg will, when the horse understands it, stop him moving his hindquarters to the right — or should the rider use it with a little more vigour or strength, it should require the horse to move his quarters AWAY — in this case to the left, the side to which we are about to require him to bend.

I repeat:

> *The drawing back of a leg to produce a lateral effect must never be allowed to interfere with the forward drive of the legs . . . never. [See Ch. 7.]*

YIELDING TO THE LATERAL LEG AIDS

Just as a horse can be easily taught to move away from a light touch of a leather rein against the side of his neck, so too can he be brought to respond to our lightest leg contacts by moving or yielding his hindquarters away from a light additional contact of the rider's drawn-back leg: provided he already answers to

LIGHT FORWARD-DRIVING AIDS.

On no account do anything to upset your horse when introducing these lessons of lateral leg aids. Use light aids, keep the horse calm and always keep in mind that if he is not doing what you want of him it means that he does not understand you. He *will* answer light lateral leg aids if you first give him the chance to learn what these new aids mean — *and then you must use light aids.*

Later in his schooling we will find that the leg aids will be superseded by changes in the weight on one or the other seat-bone. But first things first, and we will deal with how the seat is used as an aid in a later chapter [see Ch. 22 'Ultimate Aids'].

THE IMPORTANCE OF THE 'INSIDE' LEG

When we begin to use a drawn-back leg, we are naturally most concerned with the new lateral effect we will want that leg to produce. We think of the effect of the drawn-back leg — but many riders *fail to realise the importance of the leg which remains on or near the girth — THE INSIDE LEG.*

The role of the inside leg is most important.

THE INSIDE LEG
THE OUTSIDE LEG

When our right leg is drawn back and we wish to bend our horse's body to the left, the lateral effect of our left — inside — leg which still remains active near the girth, *in addition to helping the right leg maintain impulsion*, should act more or less like a post around which the rider's right leg to some degree bends the horse's body.

Unlike the drawn-back outside leg, the inside leg does not produce a great deal of **visible** lateral effect at this stage of his training. Its lateral effects might well be most commonly used to prevent the horse moving his forehand to the inside under the influence of the outside leg.

THE IMPORTANCE OF BOTH THE FORWARD AND THE LATERAL DRIVE OF THE INSIDE LEG CAN HARDLY BE EXAGGERATED.

Not only must the inside leg continue to help in maintaining impulsion but its lateral effect can prevent movement of the forelegs towards the inside should the horse show any inclination to do that [see Ch. 19 'Leg Yielding'].

Bending the horse's body could be likened to bending a length of light cane when held in both hands. Usually the two thumbs will provide the resistance around which the fingers bend the cane; but if we have any reason to do so, we can also bend the cane by pushing our thumbs in the opposite direction to that in which the fingers are pressing.

This is very similar to the role of the inside leg. Normally it is only resistant and forward-driving — but it can, by strengthening its lateral demands, push and bend the horse's forehand away from itself: in this case to the right, the outside.

Inviting the horse to "take" with the outside rein will help a good deal when introducing the lateral effects of the legs.

When changing direction or riding in circles, the lateral effect of the inside leg normally does little more than exert resistance to the outside leg, but quite often — as when riding through a corner of a manege — it commands the forelegs not to cut the corner but to keep the forehand away to the outside as well as maintain full forward drive.

We will have more to say about riding through a corner in Chapter 12, but let me remind you again that when you want to increase any leg contact you must not do so by a heavy pressure or squeezes but by means of tiny vibrations or tiny taps [see Ch. 7].

TO SUM UP

The F.E.I. Rules require the horse to bend his body to conform to the curve of the line he follows when changing direction and when making circles or part-circles.

Horses have difficulty in bending their spines to the side when first under a rider. When sufficiently advanced in training we first teach our horse the aids used to bend his body and later give him exercises that will improve his suppleness.

Both legs should produce active lateral effects when not placed opposite each other at the girth.

The lateral effect of the inside leg, although not so obvious, *is in every way* as important as that of the lateral effect of the drawn-back outside leg.

The horse has to learn to bend his spine as his forelegs and his hind legs have to step in different directions when he is changing direction. The muscles of each leg have to pull the limb to which they are attached, in slightly different directions. A suitable bend in the horse's spine will allow for this.

"At changes of direction, the horse is required to bend his body to the curvature of the line he follows, remaining supple and following the indications of the rider without any resistance or change of pace, rhythm or speed."

We first teach and practise body-bending. Only later will we ask for lateral EXERCISES.

CHAPTER 11

"ON THE BIT"

A look back over earlier schooling;
'On the bit' defined;
Importance of response to rider's leg;
"A supple poll the highest point".

The time has come for me to explain the CONDITION OF "ON THE BIT". But before I attempt this most difficult task, it might be advisable to give my reader's memory a nudge.

EARLIER SCHOOLING

You will recall how you started your young horse in his early schooling days? Turning him, you will remember, you took one rein well out to the side at first to make its meaning easy for the youngster to understand and also to give the rein the least possible stopping effect.

As soon as you could do so, you abandoned the 'open rein' and began to use the 'direct rein', which has a greater stopping effect. By that time you were able to counter the unwanted stopping effect by the use of your legs. Next followed 'Indirect rein' effects [see Ch. 18 'HORSE CONTROL — THE YOUNG HORSE'] and you then began to establish contact.

Throughout the early schooling of the horse we frequently had to 'take' or 'draw' with a rein; but the time is now approaching when we will not, under any ordinary circumstance, take or pull with either one rein or with both. *Our* days of taking or drawing on a rein are nearly over, and we now have to establish the condition known as "on the bit".

In this as in each of my other books, I have repeatedly emphasised the importance of the legs and other forward driving aids. We are now to find that with a horse 'on the bit' every movement required of him will follow only as a result of obedience to our forward driving aids.

Well ridden, a horse 'on the bit' is never asked to respond to a drawn-back rein. That 'never' might seem to be an exaggeration, but — when it occurs — a heavier rein contact will *always follow from and be the result of the rider driving the horse forward and up to the bit.*

It is the horse's response to our increased forward driving aids that will produce the changes in the rein contacts.

"ON THE BIT" DEFINED

In dressage nothing is more important than that the rider understands and recognises the feel of the condition of his horse being 'on the bit'.

I feel I cannot do better than quote the International Rules: **Article 401** defines the condition of 'on the bit':

> "In all his work, even at the halt, the horse must be 'on the bit'. A horse is said to be 'on the bit' when the neck is more or less raised and arched according to the stage of training and the extension or collection of the pace, and he accepts the bridle with a light and soft contact and submissiveness throughout.
> The head should remain in a steady position, as a rule slightly in front of the vertical, with a supple poll as the highest point of the neck, and no resistance should be offered to the rider."

'IN ALL HIS WORK...'

We find from the above rule that the condition of 'on the bit' must exist in all his work — even at the halt the horse must be on the bit . . . and 'on the bit' depends upon response to the rider's driving aids.

IMPORTANCE OF RESPONSE TO THE RIDER'S LEG

All demands upon the trained dressage horse start with the leg aids which demand forward movement; any subsequent aids we may use should result from *and only follow from* the mobility or the impulsion our legs, seat and weight aids have created [see Ch. 22 'Ultimate Aids'].

But what does it matter if the legs are used first or last — if the horse does not respond to them?

It is only after we have created impulsion [the inclination to go forward] that we are able to convert that impulse into any other action we might have in mind: circle, half-pass, pirouette, collection, extension, rein-back — anything.

We cannot get the correct results from whatever aids we propose to use unless we first FEEL the horse's attempt, his urge, his *impulse* to go forward in answer to our legs.

If the rider does not get the forward effect from the leg and seat aids, then for all practical purposes he has not used them. If the forward-driving aids have to be followed by some other aid [as they always do] then it is clear that *we cannot go on with the second effect if there has been no response to the first.*

If the horse does not answer the leg and the reins become tighter, then it is clear that the rider has pulled back on the reins instead of the horse going forward and UP TO THE BIT to feel *there* for what the bit has to tell him.

IT IS FOR THE HORSE TO GO FORWARD AND
UP TO THE BIT — NOT FOR THE RIDER TO
DRAW THE BIT BACK TO THE HORSE.

'On the bit' results only from the horse's movement up to the bit.

To almost every question we put to the late Mr Franz Mairinger, his answer was: "RIDE THE HORSE FORWARD". It is for us to add: "And up to the bit".

THE DOOR

The horse's situation is much like that of a person who stands with his two hands placed, apart, on a closed door facing him. We are going to ask him to **move forward** and, at the same time, keep the same Contact "1" feel of each hand on the door. It will not be until our friend attempts to move forward that he will find if the door is locked or not.

If the door is locked he will be able to go forward a fraction *only* if he bends his arms — and then the door will stop him.

But, if the door yields to his forward pressure, he will find that to keep an even pressure on each hand he will have to turn with the door.

We have placed our friend in much the same position as a horse when being asked to 'take' with one rein — the outside rein.

When the outside rein is springy and inviting — yielding — it invites the horse to bend his body by 'taking' or going forward with that side. The legs drive the horse up to his bit and *he finds he is invited to take with the outside rein.*

The inside hand certainly does not pull; it merely restrains.

Our horse has been taught to maintain an equal and constant contact on each rein; now he is told to step forward [or increase his impulsion] and it is not until he does so and steps 'up to the bit' that he finds what he is allowed to do:

   . . . if he meets resistance from both reins [as with the locked door] he can go up a little closer to the bit by flexing. He goes up to the bit, and if he still meets resistance he is required to halt.

   . . . if he meets less resistance on one rein than on the other, then he is required to change direction to maintain the same contact.

But — neither our friend at the door nor our horse knows what is to be required of him **until he tries to go forward when asked.**

71

WELL NAMED: "ON THE BIT"

The expression 'on the bit' has been most carefully chosen. It is more a description than a name — and aims to indicate to the rider what is to be asked of the horse.

A horse 'on the bit' does not push his nose out to find the bit. He has to be ridden forward a fraction and so get his body a little closer to the bit — and then *feel there* for whatever the bit has to tell him.

The rider may be going to ask for a change of direction or a halt, or perhaps an increase of pace — anything. If the rider lets his horse meet 'springy' hands, then it is clear the horse is required to lengthen both his neck and his stride [see Ch. 9].

If we let him meet a bit with one rein more 'springy' than the other [or, if you like, one rein more resistant than the other] then we require him to change direction. He should 'take' with the side that he finds meets least resistance . . . the rein that he finds most 'springy' . . . and this should cause him to change direction.

We may, on another occasion, let the horse meet resistance from both reins as he increases impulsion in answer to our legs. This clearly tells him that he must slow down, stop, or rein back — or later in his training, move up towards collection.

The more advanced horse must never bring his nose back — those days are over. A horse 'on the bit' does not bring his nose back closer to his body, his whole body answers to the driving aids and goes up closer — UP TO THE BIT. The same thing but with a very big difference.

"A SUPPLE POLL THE HIGHEST POINT OF THE NECK"

This might be an opportune moment to point out that going up to the bit also *takes the top of the horse's head forward a fraction* — and his doing so definitely raises his head and neck [see Fig. 20]. On the other hand, bringing his nose back just as definitely lowers his nose and tends to lower the poll [see Fig. 21].

Later in our horse's training we will require him to take his hind feet a little further forward and under his body. This, too, tends to drop or lower the hindquarters and elevate the head and neck still more — so that there should be no doubt about the poll being 'the highest point' as required **in all his work**.

Again let me remind you that the aids to be used must eventually be so light as to be invisible to an ordinary onlooker: a tiny pulsing of the driving aids and the lightest changes of rein aids. And always . . . always . . . ALWAYS . . . the light leg or other seat 'driving' aids must come first and their effects ALWAYS predominate.

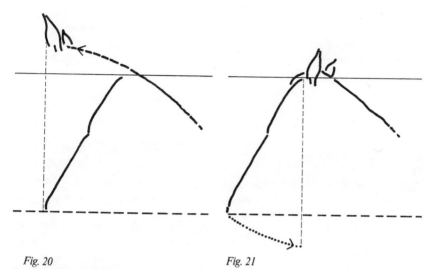

Fig. 20   Fig. 21

THE HORSE MUST GO 'UP TO THE BIT'...
Fig. 20 When the horse goes up to the bit, the bit becomes the pivot and the forward movement of the neck raises the poll.
Fig. 21 When the horse brings his nose back, the poll becomes the pivot and the bit and mouth are lowered.

We will soon face the task of teaching our horse to take his hocks, his hind feet, a little more forward — a little more under his body.

Can't you imagine the horse thinking as we gently ask him to move forward after he has already gone up to the constraint of the bit: "But I have gone forward as far as I can and you have been letting me know you were pleased with me . . . I can't go up any more . . . the bit won't let me!"

It is for us to think along the lines, gently, "Yes, dear, you have taken your body up — but you can still take your hind feet forward a fraction".

We must think kindly, for it is hard for him to see that what has pleased us up to this point, will no longer satisfy us.

Bringing the hind legs under the body slopes them and lowers the hindquarters a little; this will raise the head and neck a little, too. Later on we will introduce exercises that require our horse to flex his hind legs and place them further under his body.

DO YOU HAVE TO "PUT A BOMB UNDER HIM"?

All our careful preparations will be wasted if we do not first have the horse light to the legs. If you have to do something like 'putting a bomb under him' to get him to move with increased impulsion, it will be quite impossible to get your horse to maintain a light and constant contact with the reins.

73

I must point out that I know of no authority that claims to be able to teach a pupil the meaning of 'on the bit' without a trained horse on which to mount the pupil. To attain the higher levels of dressage you must somehow *learn to recognise the condition of 'on the bit'* and then teach it to your horse. I can only hope that you will be aided by my efforts.

I cannot stress too firmly the importance of lightness at all times. By lightness I mean immediate response by the horse to the lightest of aids: first and foremost the driving aids and then the rein aids [remember 'Tasting the Bit' in Ch. 8]. Later on even these so-light aids will be supplanted by tiny changes of balance and seat pressures.

From one lesson we advance to another, and any attempt to skip any lesson or step will reduce our horse's chance of a complete understanding of our requirements.

TO SUM UP

In early schooling the RIDER draws or 'takes' a rein: but those days are now over.

In all his work [even at a halt] the horse must be 'on the bit'. He must accept the bridle — contact — with a light and soft contact and submissiveness throughout all his work.

His neck must be more or less raised and arched according to the stage of training and the extension or collection of the pace.

His head must be steady and as a rule *slightly in front of the vertical*, with a supple poll the highest point of the neck. This means that the *nose* may be taken further forward in front of the vertical when occasion demands it — but *should never be brought back behind the vertical.*

If we ask our horse to go straight forward, our hands maintain Contact "1" and allow him to go straight on by keeping "1" on each rein.

If we want him to change direction, we invite him to 'take' with the outside rein and meet, say, "1.01" from the inside rein. As he changes direction and bends into the direction of movement, both hands and both reins return to normal Contact "1". He is doing what we asked of him and we maintain contact until we ask for another change.

For a horse to be 'on the bit', immediate and predictable responses to our driving aids are imperative.

To almost every question we put to the late Mr Franz Mairinger, his reply would be: "Ride the horse forward". It is the answer to almost every difficulty we meet.
Keep in mind the relaxed condition of "Tasting the Bit".
Never miss a chance to ride an educated horse, preferably under the eyes of a good instructor.

CHAPTER 12

RIDING A CORNER IN A DRESSAGE ARENA

Horses like to 'cut corners';
Prevention is better than correction;
Keep the horse straight;
Change the routine;
How far into a corner?
Forward drive of the inside leg.

"It's the only way I can stop him anticipating!"

Fig. 22

RIDING A CORNER IN AN ARENA

"The manner in which a rider takes his horse through the corners of a manege will clearly show the quality of his horsemanship" — the later Mr Franz Mairinger.

You will remember the Rule we quoted in Ch. 10 which makes it quite clear that "At changes of direction the horse should adjust the bend of his body to the curvature of the line he follows". Complying with that Rule makes riding a corner anything but easy — with some horses.

Almost every horse will show an inclination to 'cut in' as he nears the corner of the manege. We will be expecting him to do this, and our legs should immediately demand: "Continue straight forward".

If, at any time when we are riding on either a straight or a curved line our horse shows an inclination to move to one side, the correct action for us to take is to *drive him forward* in the direction we have had him facing. We use both legs to do that. When he goes forward in obedience to the legs we have no need to worry about his inclination to do otherwise.

The rider's aim should always be to prevent any unwanted movement rather than to correct it.

A horse that cuts a corner in a dressage test tells the judge that the rider has been slow to detect what is going on under him. The rider should be able to detect the very first inclination of his horse to move off the line he is being ridden on, and *immediately check that inclination* — not hope to get the horse back into the track a few paces later on.

The capable rider feels for the tiny changes of balance that must precede any change of direction *and by the immediate use of his legs* checks the horse's inclination before it becomes action.

It sounds easy; but most riders find it to be quite difficult.

Don't think of this cutting the corners as a deliberate disobedience on the part of the horse. He feels certain that you do want him to go around and that *you* just "put on this turn" at corners. That's why I recommend varying your demands occasionally.

KEEP THE HORSE STRAIGHT

Our task in riding a corner is first to have our horse straight as we approach the corner and then to keep him straight and moving straight on until we direct him to do otherwise.

If you find he is difficult to keep straight as you approach the corner it will almost certainly be due to your having repeatedly allowed him to 'cut in' — often with his head bent outwards. As long as he feels certain you will want him to go around the corner as you always have, he will try to cut in.

CHANGE THE ROUTINE

Until the horse's improved stage of training makes it unnecessary, it is advisable for the rider to frequently change the routine and not always continue on around every corner. For instance you can occasionally ride on and in the corner, turn about on either the forehand or the quarters and go back the way you came. Or you can ask for a rein-back or a prolonged halt just before or when you reach the corner. If you are in a suitable arena it is also a good idea sometimes to have the corners open so that you can change your mind and go straight on if your horse thinks he will start the turn when *he* likes. Do anything that is different from rounding the corner — as he has such good reason to expect you will want. Keep the young horse alert and awaiting *your orders.*

Occasionally following these lines of action will make him take more notice of your aids, although it will not alter the fact that you have not taught your horse to respond to the forward drive of your legs as you should have done *and still have to do.*

76

HOW FAR INTO THE CORNER SHOULD A HORSE BE RIDDEN?

When we can keep our young horse straight as we near a corner the next question is: when or where should we ask our horse to start the turn?

The answer will depend upon the stage of training he has reached.

Rule 409 advises: "When changing direction at a right angle, *for instance when riding corners,* the horse should describe one-quarter of a circle of approximately six metres diameter at collected or working paces".

Remember the six metres diameter [3m radius] is for a fully-trained horse. In earlier tests a much larger quarter-circle is expected [see Fig. 23]. The test is: does your horse's spine conform to the curvature of the line on which he is being ridden?

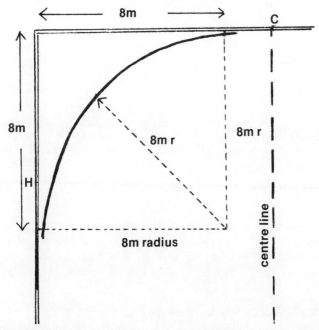

Fig. 23
In earlier tests the rider should aim at riding a quarter-circle of about 8m radius [16m diameter] as shown above. The radius should be reduced as control of the horse improves. Even the most advanced combination will not be asked to ride a circle, or part circle, of less than three metres radius [six metres diameter].

The end markers at the side of each arena are six metres from the corner. A young horse should start the turn well before reaching the marker — and when you find he is conforming to the quarter-circle you have asked, then you can begin the turn a little later. A horse that can and will make quite a good 20 metre circle often behaves badly in a corner of that size.

Be sure your quarter-circle *is* a quarter-circle; it must leave the first side and arrive at the second side at points equi-distant from the corner — it is sometimes helpful to mark the track of the corner accurately.

THE FORWARD DRIVE OF THE INSIDE LEG

So often a rider is unable to prevent his horse cutting in by just riding him forward. It is under these circumstances that such a rider usually reverts to the 'Indirect Rein' and so makes matters worse. He draws the inside rein back towards his opposite knee or hip, and endeavours *to force the horse's forelegs and shoulders outwards by the backward and sideways effect of the 'indirect rein of opposition'* [see Ch. 18 'HORSE CONTROL — THE YOUNG HORSE'].

The rider substitutes the stopping and lateral effect of the inside indirect rein of opposition for the forward drive of his legs and the lateral effect of his inside leg.

> IT IS THE INSIDE LEG, THE LEG AT THE GIRTH, THAT SHOULD — BY INCREASED FORWARD AND LATERAL DRIVE — TAKE THE HORSE'S FOREHAND OUTWARD AND SO CAUSE THE HORSE TO RESUME THE CORRECT BEND.

We must insist on our horse doing what we want him to do rather than just try to prevent him doing what HE wants to do. And remember, the judges will be looking for: "The absence of resistance or change of pace, rhythm or speed".

Lateral response to the inside leg is imperative. [Read Ch. 19, 'Leg Yielding'.]

We begin to understand what Mr Franz Mairinger meant when he said: "The manner in which a rider takes his horse through the corners of a manege will clearly show the quality of his horsemanship". There are many corners to be ridden in any test.

ALL RIGHT-ANGLE TURNS ARE NOT AT CORNERS

Where a test requires the competitor to turn across the arena at a certain marker — say 'B' — you should require your horse to begin his turn well before he reaches 'B'. A turn at a nominated marker does not mean that you are expected to ride up to that marker and then try to turn. Preliminary and Novice horses should start their turns some six to eight metres before reaching the marker at which they are required to turn, and even a fully trained horse, three metres before the marker.

Halts and turns on the hindquarters or on the forehand are different and should be made — on the spot — when the **rider's body** reaches that spot.

TURNS ON THE FOREHAND

Neither turns on the forehand nor turns on the hindquarters are mentioned in the latest F.E.I. Rulebook that I have [1979] and they no longer appear in dressage tests.

But I do recommend teaching a young horse to move away from a drawn-back leg — if only to open gates, etc.

This can be taught a horse before mounting — get him to move away from a hand tapping him just behind the girth. It plants the idea: "I have to move away from taps and pressures".

TO SUM UP

When riding through a corner or making a turn anywhere, the horse's spine is required to be bent to conform to the line on which he moves.

All horses try to cut the corners: failure to keep the horse moving straight forward until told to turn is an indication of the rider's shortcomings.

Changing the routine of riding a corner can reduce the horse's efforts to cut-in.

The rider should 'feel' for the horse's inclination to cut the corner and RIDE HIM FORWARD to prevent him doing so.

On no account should the rider revert to the use of the inside "Indirect Rein of Opposition".

Where the rider should begin his turn depends upon the stage of training the horse has reached — the degree of bend asked for at that stage.

"The manner in which a rider takes his horse through the corners of a manege will clearly show the quality of his horsemanship" . . . Franz Mairinger.

CHAPTER 13

RIDING TO A HALT

In competition many marks depend on the halt;
"A more and more restraining hand";
Standing at the halt;
"Weight to be evenly distributed";
"The poll the highest point";
Do not permit your horse to become routined;
Riding forward after the halt.

F.E.I. RULES

Every competitor in a dressage test should take care that he is fully aware of all the essentials of the halt. The halt is required at least twice in every test [when saluting the judges] and as the competitor advances into higher level, as many as six halts or more may be required in the one test. And remember . . . the very character of the halt allows the judges time to note and comment upon it.

I don't think I can do better when introducing the requirements of the halt than to quote from the rules. I will reproduce the Article as printed and remind the reader that the original is produced in French — and the official translation may not always be exactly as we would express ourselves.

Article 402 is set out in two sections:

"The halt is obtained by the displacement of the horse's weight on the quarters by a properly increased action of the seat and legs of the rider, driving the horse towards a more and more restraining but allowing hand, causing an almost instantaneous but not abrupt halt at a previously fixed place."

"At the halt, the horse should stand attentive, motionless and straight, with the weight evenly distributed over all four legs, being by pairs abreast with each other. The neck should be raised, the poll high and the head slightly in front of the vertical. While remaining 'on the bit' and maintaining a light and soft contact with the rider's hand, the horse may quietly champ the bit and should be ready to move off at the slightest indication of the rider."

Notice that a sudden or abrupt halt is not required. If we watch an experienced rider 'ride to a halt' we will see that he progressively shortens each of his horse's strides from full length to a step of perhaps only half that length and with each successive step shorter. The final step, bringing the four legs 'by pairs

80

abreast with each other', being usually not greater than a few centimetres or inches in length. The number of steps taken will depend upon the stage of training [see Fig. 24], but most important: *all steps will be forward.* On no account may the horse step back.

"A MORE AND MORE RESTRAINING HAND"

The requirement: "driving the horse forward to a more and more restraining but allowing hand", requires the rider first to lightly urge his horse forward on to the bit, and then just as lightly check the length of each stride as he feels the horse keep 'up to the bit' [see Ch. 11 and study 'On the Bit'].

An abrupt halt is clearly not required of any horse no matter how advanced his training. Even the most advanced level horse and rider will only be required to pass to an *'almost* instantaneous but not abrupt halt'.

Fig. 24
Mrs Helen Head schooling her young horse "McLaren". "McLaren" has not, at this time, been sufficiently prepared for his rider to demand he stand "all four legs being by pairs abreast with each other" but he is showing good progress: "the neck raised, the poll high, the head slightly in front of the vertical and maintaining a light and soft contact with the rider's hand . . . ready to move off at the slightest indication of the rider". Perfection is not asked for at first, but progress should be encouraged.
"McLaren" is lightly 'tasting the bit' during the halt.

A horse in a lower level test will be allowed more steps by both competitor and judges. At each step the horse has to be kept up to the bit and as he goes forward and meets the bit he finds each step he was about to take has to be constrained.

No matter how quickly or how slowly the horse is brought to a halt, the rider should always endeavour to finalise movement by a tiny step FORWARD. The horse must be driven forward into a halt. You will see now why, in this work, I place the halt after explaining "On the Bit".

STANDING AT THE HALT

Having ridden our horse 'to a halt', now let us see what is required of him when standing at a halt:

> "At the halt the horse should stand attentive, motionless and straight, with the weight evenly distributed over all four legs . . . ready to move off at the slightest indication of the rider."

From the competitor's point of view it is most important that his horse is not only ready to move off but that he gives each judge the impression he IS so ready. A horse allowed to step back clearly shows that he is anything but ready to step forward. Experienced riders are most careful not to allow the smallest *tendency* to step back — even though the rider may have over-ridden the marker where he was required to halt.

Few judges will expect a young horse to stand absolutely motionless. Nevertheless, the young horse should not be allowed to look about him as they so often are; he must SHOW attention to his rider. Keeping him motionless will help to hold his attention. Do your best to see that he stands "attentive, motionless and straight" . . . and *ready to move forward.*

DO NOT PERMIT YOUR HORSE TO BECOME ROUTINED

If, during training, there is any doubt or hesitation in getting an answer to your forward driving aids when riding to a halt, abandon all thoughts of stopping where you had intended and insist on a free response to your legs. The horse must respond without the slightest hesitation. His readiness to move forward will always be looked for by the judges when you are riding to a halt, even in the lower grade tests.

Every time a horse shows an inclination to follow any pattern or practice, make a different demand upon him. Change your routine. Remember, the judges can see every movement of the rider's legs as he rides up the centre line: driving the horse towards a more and more restraining but allowing hand' is hardly the same as hammering his ribs to keep him moving.

Occasionally we meet a horse that deliberately pokes his nose forward to increase the stopping effect of the bit. *Abandon all thoughts of stopping* if your horse tries this during schooling: insist on obedience to your driving aids. On no account continue with your intention to halt if *he* increases the weight on the reins.

WEIGHT TO BE EVENLY DISTRIBUTED OVER ALL FOUR LEGS

Now let us consider a still further requirement of the halt: "With the weight evenly distributed over all four legs, **being by pairs abreast with each other**" [see back dust-jacket].

Getting the hind legs well under the body so as to share the weight equally with the fronts is a matter of special exercises and further schooling. That will come later; but if our young horse is ridden forward to his halt and his last step is only a few centimetres, the foot last moved will hardly pass the other. They will be very close to being abreast.

When riding to the halt it is for the RIDER to check that he has his own weight well down in the saddle so that he can feel for the horse making those last tiny steps he is asked for.

Be most encouraging when the young horse responds well. He must respond to his rider's legs — for it is not until he goes up to the bit that he learns what comes next. That is why it is so important that the rider often 'changes his mind' and does not stop always in the same place when schooling. Keep him guessing — he has to be taught to stop where and when you tell him — not to stop regularly at "X" or any other spot.

The rider has to be alert *to feel for the slightest tendency* of the horse to do what is wanted of him. Always an "End of Lesson" reward must follow after each success with this, as with all lessons. The closer the rest, or other reward, follows the action we want, the sooner the horse will link them together.

THE POLL THE HIGHEST POINT OF THE NECK

When ridden to a halt a young horse will not be expected to stand collected — but riding him forward to a halt should keep his head high [see Ch. 11 "On the Bit" . . . Article 401: 'Even at the halt']. Remember too that the horse may quietly champ the bit while maintaining a light contact with the hand [Ch. 10 "Tasting the Bit".]

Note that the head is required to be slightly in front of the vertical . . . not quite vertical . . . and NEVER behind the vertical: NEVER . . . EVER . . . [see Figs. 20 and 21, Ch. 11 'On the Bit'].

RIDING FORWARD AFTER THE HALT [OR REIN BACK]

When the rider decides to continue forward after a halt — or rein-back — he must never allow the horse to move off by just lightening the reins. Your horse must wait to receive your light but clear driving aids. He has to be told: "At a walk [or when more advanced, at a trot or canter] . . . go forward".

☆ ☆ ☆

Whoever would have thought there could be so many facets to a halt — and every one of them important. Halts that fall short in any way can cost the competitor many points in a dressage test.

TO SUM UP

The halt is required at least twice in every dressage test — and many more times in more advanced tests.

The F.E.I. Rules have exacting requirements: how the horse should be ridden to a halt and how the horse should stand at a halt.

ON NO ACCOUNT should a horse be allowed to step back during a halt.

At the halt, the horse should show himself ready to move off at the required pace at the *slightest indication* of the rider. A competitor should aim to let the judges see that his horse *is* so ready.

The horse should stand "attentive, motionless and straight"; the best way to keep him attentive is to give him something to attend to.

A readiness to move forward *when required* is more important than a quick halt.

CHAPTER 14

VARIATIONS OF PACE

COLLECTED, WORKING, MEDIUM AND EXTENDED PACES

Establish a good working pace;
Lengthening the stride;
Shortening the stride;
The horse that 'runs away';
"Ride the horse forward" into less extended paces.

The International Rules set out four variations of each pace. Heading the list of variations is "collected". Each of the others is to some degree less collected, or to put it the other way, more extended: collected, working, medium and extended, in that order.

ESTABLISH A GOOD WORKING PACE

Before we think to ask our horse for a medium walk, trot or canter, we should have him moving at good working paces. He should be well up to the bit so that the hind legs are acting in obedience to the 'go-forward' aids.

We should insist on his remaining straight and maintaining absolute regularity of stride at working paces **before** asking for a longer stride [see Fig. 25]. Control the tempo of the working paces first and so make it easier for our horse to understand our demand for regularity when later we ask for longer strides. Get him 'stride conscious' at the working paces before attempting to control the stride tempo at the more difficult medium pace.

Fig. 25

"FIRST, ESTABLISH A GOOD WORKING PACE...", and this is what Mrs Helen Head is aiming for at this stage of *"McLaren's"* training. *"McLaren"* is lightly in contact and most attentive to his rider.

When you have established good working paces, the time has come to invite the horse to extend his strides a little.

LENGTHENING THE STRIDE

To lengthen his stride from a working pace to a more extended pace, our horse will need a little more rein — a slightly longer neck.

If when answering our call to extend his stride, the horse finds it necessary to stretch forward a little, he should feel free to do so.

Our failure to allow some lengthening of the neck causes the willing horse to drop each foot straight downward the last part of each extended stride. The horse is trying, but constraint of the reins will limit the necessary displacement of weight to the front. It is for the rider to permit his horse to 'take' rein a little when he drives the horse forward.

We ask for some lengthening of stride — and after a few strides we gently return him to the pace he has just left. Don't keep the increase going for long, and do not ask for it too often at first. Feel for the slightest lengthening of stride, and be ready to encourage every tendency of your horse to do as you want.

Our horse must, at all times, be 'on the bit'.

SHORTENING THE STRIDE

The order to 'take' a little and lengthen stride is followed a little later by the demand to 'give' a little and shorten stride.

If, when we are reducing the length of stride, we ride our horse 'up to the bit' by the tactful use of our legs and seat, these exercises can become one of the first moves towards collection, for the working pace is a little more collected than the medium pace.

Returning to the working pace he has just left comes easy to the horse *and he is making his first steps towards collection.*

Later on, when our horse has learnt to lengthen his stride from a working into a medium pace easily and with regularity, and he returns lightly and 'on the bit' to a working pace, we start to think to go on to a more extended pace. He will be required to lengthen stride first to a medium — and then to a more extended pace [see Fig. 26].

After each lengthening of stride, we return him to the more collected working pace.

As always, the rider should feel for the horse tasting the bit occasionally and check that he himself is relaxed and his weight well down in the saddle.

THE HORSE THAT "RUNS AWAY"

When first we drive our horse forward to get him to lengthen his stride, it is almost certain that he will not understand exactly what we want of him. The most common mistake for the horse to make is to 'run away', a term used when the horse increases the tempo of his strides instead of increasing the *length* of each stride.

When he increases the tempo in this manner it is almost impossible for the horse to step with longer strides. If, when we ask for a longer more extended stride, our horse quickens his pace and starts to 'run away', he should be immediately — but lightly — checked.

Be "with him" in this, for he has answered your forward-driving aids by increasing his impulsion; he has done *what he thinks you want*.

You should be thinking along the lines: "Not that, dear [and don't forget the 'dear'], not that". Don't be too demanding at first. Once again you are trying to introduce a new idea to him: be gentle, be considerate — and be encouraging.

Sit down in the saddle and feel for the movements of your horse's hind feet. Use your legs with short light pulsings which he will learn to associate with the movements of his hind feet. Be sure you know what you are feeling for, and be ready with voice and hand to encourage him the MOMENT HE TENDS to do as you want — step longer, and not 'run away'.

Regularity of stride must be maintained from the more collected paces to extension and back to the less extended paces. At each, the rider must feel for and note the tempo of the strides: the 1-2-3-4 of the walk; the 1-2, 1-2 of the trot, and the 1-2-3 of the canter.

"RIDE THE HORSE FORWARD" INTO LESS EXTENDED PACES

The important thing about these extensions of pace within each gait is that after each extension our horse should be gently but firmly RIDDEN FORWARD to return him to the more collected, less extended, rate.

If you are not sure as to what this entails, read again Chapter 11 "On the Bit". With a horse 'on the bit' every rein effect results from the horse's impulse to move on in answer to the rider's legs.

When your horse understands and passes to a longer stride without hesitation, start to think of 'driving him forward' to return to the working rate just as you ride him forward into a halt.

Remember, you only want your horse to lengthen to a medium stride at first. Do not ask for the extended rate until he is completely at home with the medium pace and returns lightly to the more collected working pace.

At the trot, a more extended stride should be asked of the horse only when he is moving on a straight line. At the canter a longer stride can include changes of direction.

At all paces the horse must remain 'on the bit'; the paces must remain regular, with the horse's hocks reaching well under his body.

☆   ☆   ☆

When the horse has grasped what is wanted in your arena, start to ask for some extension of the trot when out hacking. There is much to be said for asking for some lengthening of stride when trotting on slightly rising ground — horses have a natural tendency to 'spring a hill'. They not only show increased impulsion but riding up a slope requires the hind legs to be placed well under the body — so too, does riding on gentle down-hill slopes. Always be ready to encourage him on these hacking rides: tell him 'he's clever' the moment he responds correctly, or tends to do, whatever it is that you are asking of him.

Hacking can be used as a 'reward' after the 'dull' school-work — but the reward should include these straight-forward exercises.

AT THE WALK

The Rules say of the walk [Article 403.3]:

"It is at the pace of walk that the imperfections of dressage are most evident. This is also the reason why a horse should not be asked

88

to walk 'on the bit' at the early stages of training. A too precipitous collection will not only spoil the collected walk, but the medium and the extended walk as well."

For almost any purpose in life, a horse that walks well is greatly valued. See that you do all you can to encourage your horse in that most basic of all the paces, the walk. The vigour, regularity and apparent determination of a good walk always make me think of a Military March.

Only at the walk is there no 'working pace'. The prescribed paces of the walk are 'Collected', 'Medium', 'Extended', and the 'Free Walk'. We have said more about the Free Walk in Chapter 9, "Control of the Head and Neck".

The MEDIUM WALK should take the place of a working walk: and remember, a collected walk should not be asked for in a young horse's early training.

Rule 403 describes the Medium Walk as:

"A free, regular and unconstrained walk of moderate extension. The horse, remaining 'on the bit', walks energetically but calmly, with even and determined steps, the hind feet touching the ground in front of the footprints of the forefeet. The rider maintains a light, soft and steady contact with the mouth."

The Extended Walk is described as:

"The horse covers as much ground as possible, without haste and without losing the regularity of his steps, the hind feet touching the ground clearly in front of the footprints of the fore feet. The rider allows the horse to stretch out his head and neck without, however, losing contact with the mouth."

TO SUM UP

Four variations of pace are required:
COLLECTED . . . WORKING . . . MEDIUM . . . EXTENDED.

Each of the nominated paces is more extended [or less collected] than the one named before it.

In the early stages of training we will have been riding at the working or ordinary paces.

Only with the working paces well established should we ask for a slightly longer stride.

The horse should be allowed to 'take rein' a little when asked to lengthen his stride, and to lower and extend his neck and head at medium and extended paces. There should be obvious impulsion from the hindquarters.

When asked to extend his strides, the horse must not be allowed to 'run away' — increase the **tempo** of his strides.

Lengthening of the stride should be followed by a return to the more collected pace the horse has just left and its former slightly shorter length of rein.

When the horse starts to 'catch on', we should "ride him forward" into the more collected pace as required by the rule for the halt: the rider gently using his legs and seat to drive the horse up to a "more and more restraining hand".

At loose rein work the horse should maintain the pace and the direction set.

At a Free Walk the horse is allowed complete freedom to lower and stretch out his head and neck, but the reins should maintain contact [see Ch. 9].

A Free Walk is asked for in the very earliest tests and should be one of our first goals.

CHAPTER 15

YOUR FIRST DRESSAGE TEST

Get to the competition ground early;
The parade past the judges;
How best to get a straight entrance;
Saluting the judges: time allowed;
Errors of the course; Riding a corner;
Learning your Test;

I would like to say a few words that might prove helpful to riders about to enter their first dressage test — for knowing the 'tricks of the trade' can prove useful in events of any kind.

TIME TO LOOK AROUND

First, get to the site of the competition in good time to look around and see if there is anything near the arena that might upset your horse — anything strange that he might not have seen before.

If you are taking a horse to a show for the first time, get on him when you are there and move around for only a few minutes. Then put him away again. Do that several times if you can. Ask little or nothing from him in these short walks. The thing is to leave in his mind the thought: "There's nothing to it". If a sight, sound, situation, company, condition, demand or anything at all, is novel — it will lose its fearfulness much more quickly if you terminate it before anything has a chance to go wrong. It becomes "Old Hat".

Perhaps I should mention here that on no account may you enter the dressage arena before the competition starts, so do the next best thing and let your horse see the tape or chain and markers from the outside of the dressage ring. Quietly walk around the outside of the arena before the tests begin — if you can.

PARADE PAST THE JUDGES

When it is your turn to compete next, walk around the outside of the ring, quite close to the tapes and markers and pass in front of the judges in their judging boxes so that they may see your gear etc. After you have passed them, quietly turn about and walk back letting the judges see your other side as well as your number, should you be wearing one.

Take advantage of this required parade past the judges and so reduce the chance of your horse shying at them or their boxes when you are riding your test.

YOU ARE NEXT TO GO...

After your parade, trot quietly back to the entrance end of the arena and there keep your horse trotting while waiting for the bell to call you into the ring. You are required to enter within one minute of the bell or whistle. If your horse is a quiet dreamy sort, wake him up a little.

ALLOW FOR YOUR HORSE'S NATURAL BEND

Every horse has a tendency to bend much more freely to one side than to the other, or to put it in different words he is more difficult to straighten up from that side. Your horse is not likely to be an exception, so before entering the arena have him trotting in a nice-sized circle on the rein to which he does *not* bend easily — for from that side he will be most easily straightened to enter the ring. Most horses bend more easily to the right and the rider of such a horse should trot his circles on the left rein. Make the circle in such a position that you have only to straighten him to have him directly in line with the centre-line of the arena at the entrance [see Fig. 27].

The point is to have your horse straight and stepping forward with impulsion before he enters the arena and comes under the judges.

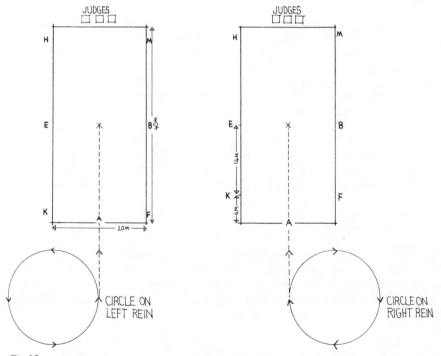

Fig. 27
Placing your horse to make the most advantageous entrance.

92

ENTER, HALT AND SALUTE THE JUDGES

Enter the ring at the trot [or specified pace] and your next concern is the halt and the salute to the judges.

The important thing about the halt is for the rider to remember that the horse should show willingness and readiness to go forward. The slightest step to the rear usually results in a very low mark [see Ch. 13 'Riding to a Halt'].

Time allowed: do not hurry your salute to the judges. Although judging begins the moment you enter the ring and continues until you leave again at "A", time is taken — the watch is started — only when you move on *after the first salute*, and it is stopped when the competitor *salutes the judges after the final halt*.

To salute the Judges: lady competitors pass both reins into one hand, allowing the other hand to drop to the full extent of the arm. She should then acknowledge the judges by gently nodding or inclining her head — as she would to acknowledge a friend — without lowering her eyes or hurrying in any way. Having saluted, she takes a rein in each hand and rides on again at the required pace.

A gentleman rider should pass both reins into one hand, remove his hat and drop his free hand, still holding his hat, to the full length of his arm. After a slight pause, he replaces his hat and rides forward after taking a rein in each hand. It is most important that the feel on the reins is quite even, so that the horse keeps his head straight and moves off on a straight line. He must not move until given the aids by the rider: "Walk, or trot, on".

Most competitors pass the reins into their left hand; the F.E.I. Rules require: "Take the reins in one hand". The whip, if carried, must be held in the same hand as the reins for the salute.

Do not hurry your salute. Remember, time is not a consideration.

ERRORS OF THE COURSE

If you make a mistake when riding your test, on no account let your mind dwell on your error. If you are confused about what you should be doing next, ride up to the judges when the bell is rung and the Chief Judge will direct you. Never worry about the mistake made. Everyone makes a mistake or two at times and the important things for you to think about are the movements yet to come.

In any exercise that must be carried out at a certain point of the arena, it should be done at the moment when *your body* is at that point.

CIRCLES — NOT 'OVALS'

You are almost certain to be required to ride at least two 20-metre circles in your test. Be sure you don't let your horse cut-in when making these circles. He should go right out into the track for a pace or two at each side and also at the end of the arena.

Then — as if you haven't enough to think about — repeatedly check your position and appearance. Look up and stretch up: "Down the weight" and "Upright the body".

RIDING THE CORNERS

Each corner is a quarter-circle, and the horse's body should be bent around the rider's inside leg. Ride well into each corner and keep in mind that in all such changes of direction, your horse is required to bend his body so that his spine conforms to the curvature of the line he follows.

Most young horses try to cut the corner. Always — and in this matter particularly — we aim to prevent a wrong move rather than to correct it. To do this we have to anticipate the horse's inclination to cut the corner of the arena: our aim should be to ride into each corner as far as the horse's ability to bend his body will allow [see Ch. 12 'Riding a Corner'].

LEARNING YOUR TEST

There are many riders unwilling to undertake a first dressage test because they have to commit it to memory. In some cases the tests are allowed to be called; but this can sometimes be most unsatisfactory — on windy days, for instance.

Fig. 28

LEARNING YOUR TEST

"Each rider has his own method of memorising a test . . ." Lorraine Micke shows how Mum can also get some housework done!

I have often been asked for 'an easy way to learn a test', and I can usually help the enquirer by pointing out that each pace of walk, trot and canter, is judged first on one rein and then on the other. Movements such as down the long side, along the end and then across the arena can be visualised as a sort of 'safety-pin' shape; there are 'U' shapes and circles. Each rider has his own method of memorising a test. At a school I held in Victoria on one occasion I was most amused to see a group of the youngsters, test sheets waving in their hands, trotting and cantering the test on their own two feet. It was most effective, too.

But you are at the test ground now. Do the best you can with your horse and try to make the test an enjoyable sport. Do try to give the judges a smile as you salute.

TO SUM UP

Get to the competition ground early and accustom your horse to the place.

When it is your turn to compete, parade past the judges. Let them see both sides of you and your horse — and let your horse have an opportunity to see the judges in their boxes.

Trot back to the entrance end of the arena and while waiting for the bell to call you, get your horse loosened up and placed so that you have the best chance of making a straight entrance.

Have your horse straight and showing impulsion when riding to a halt; and be sure he does not step back even the smallest possible step.

Salute the judges and remember there is nothing to be gained by hurrying the salutes.

Do not let your horse cut-in, either when making circles or when riding through the corners.

Remember what you have been told about position in the saddle: "Down the weight: Upright the body". Check repeatedly for stiffness.

As you ride a movement, three things should be in your mind:
   1] *What does the movement ask?*
   2] *How are we — you and your horse — carrying it out?*
   3] *What is the next movement and where does it start?*

If you make a mistake and cannot remember what movement comes next — ride to the Chief Judge and he will direct you.

REMEMBER — dressage is sport and fun.

CHAPTER 16

THE COUNTER-CANTER

Introducing the counter-canter;
Begin by asking only a little;
Why the counter-lead?

THE COUNTER-CANTER [SOMETIMES CALLED THE CONTRA-CANTER OR FALSE CANTER]

I feel I cannot do better than quote the Rules for this requirement.

Rule 405.5 states: "This is a movement where the rider, for instance on a circle to the left, deliberately makes his horse canter with the right canter lead [with the off-fore leading].

"The counter-canter is a suppling movement. The horse maintains his natural flexion at the poll to the outside of the circle, in other words is bent to the side of the leading leg. His conformation does not permit the spine to be bent to the line of the circle."

"The rider, avoiding any contortion causing contraction and disorder, should especially endeavour to limit the deviation of the quarters to the outside of the circle, and restrict his demands according to the degree of suppleness of the horse."

We can 'boil that down' as far as our horse is concerned to: the horse has to canter on the wrong lead to his rider's demand. When on the counter-canter, the horse should maintain his natural bend at the poll towards the side of the leading leg — and the rider is required to limit the movement of the hind legs to the outside of the circle or curved line on which the horse is asked to move.

The rules speak of the counter-lead *on circles*, and again, as always, the rules speak of what is required of the trained horse — but we are dealing with a young horse still in his early schooling.

INTRODUCING THE COUNTER-CANTER

As with every other lesson, we ask for little at first.

The first counter-lead is asked for in the present Novice Dressage Test. In this test, a rider is cantering his horse around the arena on the left rein and with the near-fore leading. As he approaches the 'H' marker, the test requires:

"From 'H' to 'K' serpentine one loop of 5 metres in from the track without change of leg" [See Fig. 29].

The serpentine of one loop forms a long curve with a very small bend in it, and if we don't worry too much about his hindquarters moving outwards the first few times we ask our horse for this counter-lead, little difficulty will be experienced with it.

From this test on, the serpentines — or lines curved from left to right and right to left — become more and more demanding.

In this first serpentine we should not ask for perfection; we aim only to plant the idea in our horse's mind that he is required NOT to change leg. Only later need we become more exacting about the required bend at the poll and the restraint of the quarters. As usual we become more demanding as our horse makes progress and shows his understanding.

The requirement in the rules, "the horse is bent to the side of the leading leg", means that [like the Shoulder-in] the horse has to be bent away from the direction in which he is required to move. Getting that flexion at the poll usually gives little trouble, for as the rule tells us "His conformation does not permit the spine to be bent to the line of the circle" when on the counter-canter.

Limiting the movement of the quarters to the outside of the circle is much more difficult, and the demands made in later tests will be graded so as to progressively improve the horse's ability to deal with sharper bends. We cannot prevent the deviation of the quarters to the outside of the circle and we are not asked to do so. All that the rule asks for is that the rider: " . . . should specially endeavour to *limit* the deviation of the quarters to the outside of the circle . . .".

In the particular test instanced, we have just ridden around the corner of the manege on the left rein. We have had our right leg drawn back to keep the horse's quarters in and his head will be flexed to the left.

It is clear that for this counter-lead our right leg will need to be brought forward to its near-the-girth position so that we can, with both legs, "ride the horse forward".

We should not draw the left leg back in an effort to 'limit the deviation of the quarters to the outside of the counter-canter bend', for this could cause our horse to change leg. Just ride the horse forward with both legs at the girth and keep the natural flexion at the poll to the outside of the bend.

Occasionally we meet a young horse that repeatedly changes his leading foreleg when first asked to do a counter-lead. I have found the best corrective for this little trick is not to change to a trot or walk and try to start off again on a counter-lead but IMMEDIATELY ride him around on a fairly small circle — to the left in the case we are dealing with. This means that he profits not at all from his change of lead — and we then try him again on the curved line or serpentine he was on.

REQUIREMENTS BECOME MORE DEMANDING

In the next-level test, the Elementary, a more demanding serpentine is asked for, i.e.:
"At 'A', serpentine three loops without change of leg three metres

97

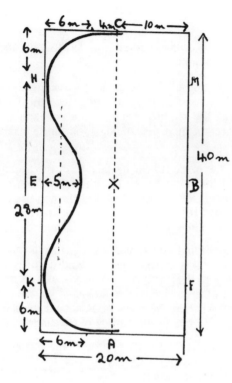

Fig. 29A

In a serpentine that bends 5 metres in the distance 'H' to 'K' as shown above, only half that bend is counter-canter.

Fig. 29B

In the next test the bend of the serpentine is increased as shown above. In later tests, much more demanding counter-canters will be required.

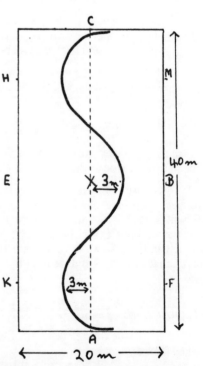

98

each side of the centre-line finishing at 'C'''.

The first and third bends are each of 3 metres and the second bend is also of 3 metres — but the horse is required to maintain a counter-lead when dealing with it.

First we introduce these easy serpentines without change of lead; then we go on until the bends become half-circles and circles. Eventually we come to require our horse to strike off on the counter-lead on a circle.

Our aim should include making the horse very conscious of the aids that tell him which leg he is to lead with at the canter.

In all early work we insisted on our horse leading only with the correct leg. Next we required him not to change leg on small bends and serpentines — and we have made the bends of the serpentines progressively sharper and sharper. Then follows our demand to strike off at the counter-lead.

All these exercises lead up to a flying change of leg with a change of direction: and finally to flying changes of leg when riding on a straight line.

ON NO ACCOUNT hurry the counter-canter lessons.

They should be spread over many months. The flying change will not be asked for until much later in his training [see Ch. 23, "The Flying Change"].

TO SUM UP

At the counter-canter the horse has to canter on the wrong lead to his rider's demand.

At first ask for only a few strides of counter-canter on a curve or serpentine loop with only a small bend.

Both the rider's legs should be positioned near the girth for the counter lead and the rider 'ride his horse gently forward'.

From riding slightly curved lines we ask for more and more until eventually we require circles on the counter lead.

These exercises make the horse very conscious of the leading leg and increase his suppleness.

DO NOT HURRY THE COUNTER-CANTER LESSONS . . . WHICH LEAD UP TO THE "FLYING CHANGE" — LATER.

CHAPTER 17

PART I: THE REIN BACK
(... would be better termed "The Ride-Back")

First halt correctly;
ON NO ACCOUNT use force or a heavy hand;
Difficult horses.

PART II: THE HALF-HALT
(another misnomer)

International Rules;
"Prepare to ..."

THE REIN BACK

Before I go on I would like to say that unlike the expression "On the bit", I have always thought the term "rein-back" tends to mislead. "Step-back" or "Ride-back" would perhaps be more appropriate. "Rein back" suggests pulling or drawing back — no matter how lightly — on the reins.

It is quite easy to teach a horse to step backwards even months before he is ridden. Read in Chapter 4 "HORSE CONTROL — THE YOUNG HORSE", how even in his earliest days before he is ridden, the young horse is required to yield to a stretched rope or rein and either lead forward or step to either side — or step back.

The rein-back of dressage is much more demanding, it is true, but anything we can introduce before a horse is ridden helps toward an easier understanding when we are mounted.

FIRST: HALT CORRECTLY

In dressage a good deal more is asked for in the rein back than just moving backwards.

First see that you have a satisfactory halt with all its requirements — particularly that the horse is 'ready to move off at the slightest indication of the rider'.

Here are some of the requirements of the rein back as in the 1979 F.E.I. Rules:

"... the feet should be raised and set down in diagonal pairs;
... each forefoot should be raised and set down an instant before the diagonal hind foot;
... on hard ground, sometimes four separate beats are clearly audible."

Anticipation of the rein-back, or evasion of the hand, the quarters moving off a straight line, spreading or inactive hind legs or dragging fore feet, are serious faults in a dressage test rein-back.

100

The horse is required to be "On the bit", which means among other things that in a dressage rein-back the horse should not know until he picks his feet up whether he will be required to move forward — or back.

Remember, it is not until the horse "goes up to the bit" **in response to the legs** that he finds out what directions the reins will have for him.

DIFFICULT HORSES

If, when you ask your horse to step back you fail to get the required movement to the rear, it will be because the horse does not understand what is wanted of him. ON NO ACCOUNT USE FORCE OR A HEAVY HAND.

Go back to the dismounted lesson of yielding to a stretched rein or rope set out on pp.. 21-26 of "HORSE CONTROL — THE YOUNG HORSE".

Nothing is more important than keeping the horse calm and relaxed: do not try to force these first steps to the rear. Walking backwards is not a natural movement for the horse, and *extra weight on the hindquarters increases his difficulties*. Make a point of not overloading the quarters when executing the movement: on no account should the rider lean back during a rein-back.

☆   ☆   ☆

In training, care should be taken to avoid letting your horse become routined to stepping back a certain number of steps by reason of that number being asked for in a certain test. Vary the number. **Do not let your horse become "routined".**

The horse should never be halted after a rein-back; always, ALWAYS the horse must be ridden forward following a rein-back and throughout the exercise he must show his READINESS to step forward.

☆   ☆   ☆

TO SUM UP: PART I

In view of the requirements of the rules, the terms 'step back' or 'ride back' would be more appropriate than 'rein back'.

To move backward in answer to a stretched rein or rope should have been introduced to the young horse before he is ridden.

The rules describe the rein-back as "An equilateral, retrograde movement". Any tendency on the part of the horse to be in any way uneven in his steps to the rear, or any tendency to evade the bit or be other than keen to move on, is considered to be a serious fault.

The horse should be "On the bit" both at the preceding halt and during every step of the rein-back.

CHAPTER 17

PART II: THE HALF-HALT

An inappropriate term;
International Rules;
"Prepare to . . . "

"HALF-HALT" AN INAPPROPRIATE TERM

Article 408 of the International Rules tells us:

> "The half-halt is a hardly visible, almost simultaneous, co-ordinated action of the seat, the legs and the hands of the rider, with the object of increasing the attention and balance of the horse before the execution of several movements or transitions to lesser and higher paces. In shifting slightly more weight on to the horse's quarters, the engagement of the hind legs and the balance on the haunches are facilitated, for the benefit of the lightness of the forehand and the horse's balance as a whole".

That is the 'half-halt' — and surely a term such as 'the prepare' should be more fitting than the 'half-halt'.

But call it what they like, the object of the half-halt is to increase the attention and balance of the horse **in preparation for a new demand**: very much like a Sergeant-Major giving orders to his Company to get them to move in unison. He makes a point of WARNING the men so that they will all move in unison as required . . . he bawls out:

"Company . . . [pause] . . . HALT";
or: "Company . . . [pause] . . . right . . . [pause] . . . TURN".

And that is what a half-halt is meant to do: warn our horse to be prepared for a demand we are about to make on him.

THE HALF-HALT IS A WARNING TO OUR HORSE
TO PREPARE FOR AN ORDER TO FOLLOW.

This warning should consist of something like a vibration on the reins together with the judicious use of the driving aids. That's for the horse — but the *rider* should also check his own position and condition. Is he relaxed? Is he, himself, prepared for the change he is about to ask of his horse?

Certainly there should be no check in the horse's pace as the term, 'half-halt' suggests. Notice that the official definition puts the **driving aids** first, and the "almost simultaneous" use of the hands follows.

The rider is really telling his horse: "Get ready . . .", or "Prepare . . .". Perhaps the latter term would be more appropriate than 'half-halt'; in any case, I recommend riders to think of it as such.

'LIGHTNESS OF THE FOREHAND"

The half-halt can also be used to correct a horse that tends to put too much weight on his forehand — and leans on the bit to do so.

The vibrations of a half-halt makes the bit an uncomfortable head-rest — and tends to make the horse transfer weight on to his quarters.

☆   ☆

HALF-HALT = GET READY = PREPARE

☆   ☆   ☆

TO SUM UP

The term 'half-halt' means the almost simultaneous use of the driving and restraining aids used to prepare the horse for a demand about to be made on him.

'Half-halt' really means: "ATTEND TO ME . . . BE PREPARED . . . BE READY".

The horse's paces should not be shortened as the term 'half-halt' seems to imply. It should only warn the horse of a demand about to be made.

The rider should check his own position and balance and the condition of his muscles to see that he himself is not stiff.

Any action of the reins should be very light; not more than a vibration.

The vibration on the bit tends to cause the horse to transfer a little weight to his quarters, slightly lightening his forehand.

CHAPTER 18

MIS-USE OF THE DOUBLE BRIDLE

Double bridle can cause difficulties;
The bridoon rein slips;
Shorten bridoon rein only;
Danger of over-bent neck.

*[See Frontispiece "HORSE CONTROL AND THE BIT" for details of a
well-fitted double bridle; read Chapter 12 for correct fitting of curb bits, chains,
etc. Be sure you know WHY the bit and rein should act at a 90° angle.]*

THE DOUBLE BRIDLE CAN CAUSE TROUBLE

In higher level dressage tests where a double bridle is required to be used,
one often sees a number of over-bent horses: horses with the highest point of their
neck many centimetres back from their poll. Yet a horse 'on the bit' is required to
work and even halt with the "poll the highest point of the neck".

In competitions of this standard this trouble is almost always due to the
rider having too much weight on the bottom rein — the curb rein — or to put it
another way he has **the bottom rein too short, too tight**.

Almost invariably the rider starts off with his reins carefully and correctly
adjusted for length: that is, with the top or bridoon rein a trifle shorter than the
bottom or Bit rein — but he *fails to maintain the adjustment*.

This leads to the question: "What tension should there be on the Bit rein of
a double bridle?"

And my answer to that question is: "None".   [See Fig. 30A.]

The rider will have done all his riding on a snaffle up to the time of starting
his horse on the double bridle, and although he now has to begin to use a double
bridle he should continue to *ride* on the snaffle — the bridoon.

THE BRIDOON REIN WILL SLIP

Almost always the rider starts off with each rein correctly adjusted for
length but during the period in which he rides to prepare his horse to enter the ring,
we find the bridoon rein slips through his fingers a little — and it *will* slip until it
becomes the same length as the Bit rein.

The RIDER has unintentionally brought the Bit and its curb into action.
The rein has to slip only a fraction of an inch — a centimetre or so — for this to
happen.

SHORTEN BRIDOON REIN ONLY

I stress that it is the bridoon rein that slips and becomes longer, and it is the bridoon rein ONLY that needs to be shortened again.

We find the bridoon rein — the top rein — *will* slip, notwithstanding that saddlers always make it a little wider than the Bit rein. This does make it a little easier to hold — but we find it still slips and then the Bit brings the horse's nose in too far.

Almost always the rider realises that his horse has become overbent and is no longer "On the bit" — but he evidently fails to recognise where the fault lies.

Instead of shortening the bridoon rein only and RIDING THE HORSE FORWARD, only too often he raises his hands — and takes them forward too — in a futile endeavour to raise his horse's head back into the correct position. The higher the hands are raised and the further forward the hands are taken, *the more the Bit rein is stretched and tightened.*

The willing horse then brings his nose even further back in an effort to act on the instruction of the curb Bit. Raising the hands actually *increases* the weight on the already over-tight Bit rein.

The rider must readjust his reins and ride on the bridoon: for it is one of the tasks of the bridoon — the snaffle — to elevate the horse's head and keep it elevated.

The Bit — the curb — should only come into action when the horse puts his nose out past the angle his rider has in mind. A too-tight Bit rein will lower the horse's head and bring his nose back towards his chest: he becomes OVERBENT AND BEHIND THE BIT.   [See Figs. 30B and 30C.]

"THE ONLOOKER SEES MOST OF THE GAME..."

Riders should check all these facts for themselves. Watch others and see how obvious these things are to the onlooker.

Discipline yourself to shorten the bridoon rein the moment you feel your horse start to overbend. Remember, by raising your hands you are not only advertising to everyone that your horse is no longer 'On the bit' but no judge could possibly give high marks to anyone riding with their hands held so high and so far forward.

LOOSENING THE CURB CHAIN IS NOT THE ANSWER

Many riders show they KNOW it is the curb Bit that is bringing their horse's nose back, and in an effort to neutralise it they ride with a curb chain fitted much too loosely. *It is not the curb chain that needs lengthening — it is the curb rein.*

FAMILIARISE YOURSELF WITH DOUBLE REINS

I recommend all riders approaching the double bridle stage to make themselves at home with the double bridle REINS before starting to use the double bridle itself. Learn to maintain their relative lengths at first on a snaffle only, but use the proper set of double bridle reins: top rein a little wider than the bottom.

Fig. 30A
Mr Les Szathmary-Kiraly,
Dressage Instructor, Dressage
Club of South Australia,
demonstrates the correct use of
the double bridle. The bottom
Bit — curb — rein is passive.

Learn, too, to recognise the feel of the wider bridoon rein so that you can find it by feel alone when you need to make a re-adjustment, without looking down.

Keeping the head carried high is still the task of the bridoon, as it has been throughout training. The Bit rein should only come into action when the horse attempts to take his nose out — further forward — than the rider requires.

Should you have doubts about riding on the bridoon alone when using a double bridle, I suggest you look closely at pictures of the hands of some of the great riders of days past. In some of them you will see only the right bridoon rein in the right hand: in the other hand you will see three reins, the left bridoon rein and the two Bit reins. Surely this makes it clear that they did not RIDE on the Bit.

Fig. 30B
The horse pokes his nose out —
and automatically the correctly
adjusted Bit rein is brought into
action.

They utilised it but did not ride on it.

The role of the Bit is a passive one with the double bridle.

Fig. 30C
This time, holding the two Bit reins in one hand, Mr Szathmary-Kiraly shows what can — and usually does — result from a too tight Bit rein. The horse, in his efforts to respond to the pressure of the curb-chain, brings his nose back with his face well behind the vertical. [See again Fig. 20 and Fig. 21.]

TO SUM UP

If the Bit rein of a double bridle is held at the same length or shorter than the bridoon rein it causes the horse to bring his nose in too far and lowers his neck — and he is no longer 'On the bit'.

It is not enough to start off with the bridoon rein a little shorter [as it should be] for it *will* slip through the fingers.

The reins of a double bridle need to be continually checked and where necessary repeatedly re-adjusted, so that the Bit rein remains a trifle longer than the bridoon rein.

Raising the hands and carrying them forward in an effort to correct the head carriage when the bottom rein is too tight is more than futile: it makes matters worse.

The role of the Bit of a double bridle is a passive one. It should come into action only when the horse 'pokes his nose' forward past the angle the rider requires. Taking the nose too far forward should bring the curb into action; correction of that movement should bring relief from its action.

The so small difference in rein length must be most rigorously maintained.

CHAPTER 19

*[This, with the following three chapters, will be of interest
mainly to the more serious dressage rider.]*

LATERAL MOVEMENTS AND EXERCISES:
LEG-YIELDING AND SHOULDER-IN

*Lateral movements and exercises;
Why yield to the 'inside leg'?
Introducing leg-yielding;
Leg-yielding leads to shoulder-in;
Summing up leg-yielding;
Starting the shoulder-in;
Don't hurry;
Importance of re-asserting free forward movement.*

LATERAL MOVEMENTS AND EXERCISES

Lateral movements are those in which all four legs of the horse are required
to move to the same side. These movements comprise the five listed below:

...Leg-yielding
...Shoulder-in
...Travers
...Renvers
...Half-pass

and they do not include the pirouette, in which the pivoting foot should not move
to either side.

This might be a good time to draw attention to Rule 411 of the F.E.I.
Dressage Rules, which includes:

> **"At all lateral movements** the side to which the horse
> should be bent is the inside. The opposite side is the
> outside."

Note that this sub-section of Rule 411 applies to lateral movements
only.

In Chapter 10 we dealt with the body-bending aids necessary for us to be
able to get our horse to 'adjust his spine to the curvature of the line he is following'.
But those were merely body-bending demands — and certainly not lateral
exercises.

The horse now understands his rider when he uses a drawn-back leg to bend
his horse's body when moving on circles or through a corner — and the time has
come to introduce him to lateral exercises: exercises that will move both fore and
hind legs toward the same side.

The first of these, leg-yielding, is anything BUT body-bending.

☆   ☆   ☆

LEG-YIELDING

It is interesting and I think instructive, that leg-yielding — the lateral response to the INSIDE leg — is the first of the lateral exercises required to be taught.

The Rules tell us:

> "In leg-yielding the horse **is quite straight**, except for a slight bend at the poll, so that rider is just able to see the eyebrow and nostril on the inside. The inside legs pass and cross in front of the outside legs. The horse is looking away from the direction in which he is moving.
>
> Leg-yielding is the most basic of all lateral movements and should be included in the training of the horse before he is ready for collected work."

Leg-yielding can be performed 'on the diagonal', in which case the horse should be as close as possible parallel to the long side of the arena, although the forehand should be *slightly* in advance of the quarters. It can also be performed 'along the wall', in which case the horse should be at an angle of about 35° to the direction in which he is moving. [See Figs 31-33.]

The Rules mention that *'leg-yielding is the most basic of all lateral movements'* — i.e. *the base from which all lateral movements commence.* Yielding to the INSIDE leg comes FIRST in lateral exercises.

WHY YIELD TO THE INSIDE LEG?

Leg-yielding is the only lateral exercise in which the horse is not required to bend uniformly from poll to tail. The horse has to be quite straight except for a very slight bend at the poll . . . WHY?

Leg-yielding — as an exercise — introduces the horse to the demands of the rider's inside leg with the least possible distraction of other aids.

The body-bending exercises with which he is now familiar, stress and draw attention to the requirements of a drawn-back outside leg. Now follows leg-yielding — which ensures that neither horse nor rider overlooks the **importance of the inside leg** as an aid — the leg that remains at the girth — the leg that is NOT drawn-back.

Leg-yielding aims to ensure that the importance of the lateral effect of the inside leg is not over-looked or under-rated. DO NOT DRAW THE OUTSIDE LEG BACK WHEN PRACTISING LEG-YIELDING.

What the Rule wants to tell us is: "The horse's back is straight: leave it straight for this exercise".

Remember, you have taught your horse to bend his body in response to a drawn-back outside leg. On no account should you draw back the outside leg in

109

this exercise where the horse has to keep his back and body quite straight.

Yielding to the inside leg — the leg at the girth — is the lesson of 'leg-yielding'.

INTRODUCING LEG-YIELDING

It will be seen that leg-yielding can be performed 'on the diagonal', and it is suggested that this is the best way to introduce it to our horse [see Fig. 31]. There is much to be said for this practice, which is much simpler for the horse — and so it is recommended. 'On the diagonal' from the wall can then follow and last of all, the horse can be asked for the movement 'along the wall'.

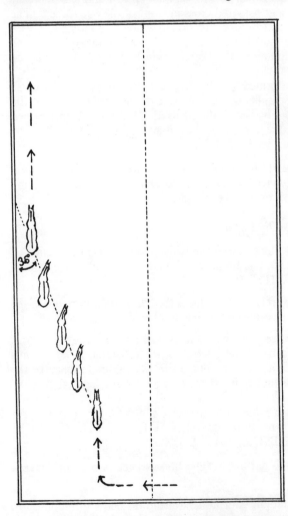

Fig. 31
STARTING LEG-YIELDING
This diagram illustrates the suggested introduction to leg-yielding. The drawing shows the horse moving towards the left side of the arena with the head SLIGHTLY bent away from the direction of movement. The forehand should be slightly in front of the quarters.
The horse has to move sideways, with a quite straight spine except for that so small bend at the poll, and has to move at an angle not exceeding 35°: which means 35° or less, and I recommend you make it a much smaller angle than that at first.

As you work in your manege, ride your horse on to the short side of the arena, pass the centre-line and then before reaching the long side, turn right [if you are on the right rein]. When ready and straight, ask your horse to leg-yield to your right leg and move forward *and* sideways to his left. The leg should be used with light throbs or 'pulsings' as described in Chapter 7.

Your horse will be straight and about parallel with the long side and he now has to learn to yield to his rider's right, or 'inside' leg — which will, when he understands it, cause him to move on a diagonal line towards the track on the long side, while still maintaining a straight body.

When so moving, diagonally to his left, the horse should have a slight bend at the poll so that he looks *away* from the direction in which he is moving. This means that the right side is the 'inside' when leg-yielding to the left . . . but remember, the *bend at the poll* should be only enough for the rider to be 'just able to see the eye-brow and nostril on the inside': the eyebrow, not the eye.

The advantage of introducing leg-yielding on the diagonal as above is that it takes advantage of the horse's natural inclination to return to the long side of the arena. Ask for a much smaller angle than 35° at first, but the horse's body must be quite straight. [See Figs 32 and 33.]

Leg-yielding aims to impress upon both horse and rider the importance of the 'inside' leg aid. In later work, its sideways — lateral — effect is not conspicuous . . . not easily seen . . . but it must be there.

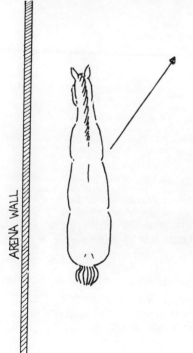

ARENA WALL

"LEG-YIELDING ON THE DIAGONAL FROM THE SIDE OF THE SCHOOL"

Fig. 32
The straight back of the horse should be at an angle of *NOT MORE THAN 35°* to the direction of movement. We have recommended you introduce leg-yielding on the diagonal from about the quarter-line towards the side of the school.
As the horse's understanding grows, follow that with leg-yielding FROM the side of the school as shown and then by leg-yielding along the side or wall as shown in the next figure.

Remember the rule: "LEG-YIELDING IS THE MOST BASIC OF ALL LATERAL MOVEMENTS".

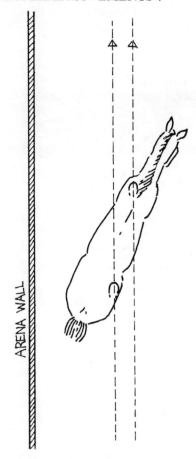

Fig. 33
LEG-YIELDING ALONG THE WALL
The horse should move at an angle of about 35° — eventually. The inside legs pass and cross in front of the outside legs. Note the very small flexion at the poll: in the movement shown the rider should just see the eyebrow and nostril on the inside. The horse's back should be quite straight.

ARENA WALL

TO SUM UP: LEG-YIELDING

Each exercise should introduce the next, making it easier for the horse to understand.

Leg-yielding teaches the horse to move away from the rider's inside leg — practically nothing more than that. It could not be more simple. It is the horse's first introduction to a lateral exercise. He is not asked or permitted to bend his body.

The horse should move at an angle of about 35°.

The objective of leg-yielding is to introduce the horse to the lateral demands of the **inside leg** with the least possible distraction of any other aid.

Now let us move on from that base to:

THE SHOULDER-IN

LEG-YIELDING LEADS TO SHOULDER-IN

Once the horse has completely mastered leg-yielding — yielding to our inside leg — he is ready for the shoulder-in, which will require him to yield to both our inside leg AND our drawn-back outside leg.

Unlike leg-yielding, in which the horse's body has to be "quite straight" except for a very slight bend at the poll, the shoulder-in exercise requires the horse to be *slightly bent around the inside leg of the rider* at an angle of about 30°.

As with leg-yielding, the horse has to be bent AWAY FROM THE DIRECTION OF MOVEMENT [see Fig. 34].

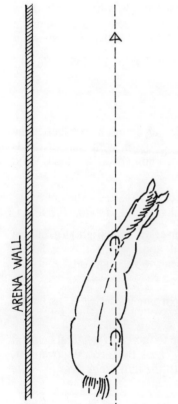

ARENA WALL

Fig. 34
RIGHT SHOULDER-IN ALONG THE WALL
At a glance this figure appears very similar to that of leg-yielding along the wall. Actually the only similarity is the bend in each case AWAY from the direction of movement — or as they are both lateral movements, the horse is bent to the inside in each case.
In leg-yielding the horse has to be quite straight except for the so-small bend at the poll.
IN SHOULDER-IN the horse has to be SLIGHTLY bent around the rider's inside leg.
In leg-yielding the inside legs cross in front of the outside legs.
IN SHOULDER-IN the forehand is slightly bent in FROM the hinds, which move along the track as for normal forward movement.
This sketch is copied from the Rule Book and shows the hindquarters moving along the track in their normal position. This is as it should be, for the horse's spine has to be bent from the hindquarters — only the fore-legs are required to move to the inside — and the diagram shows this. The outside foreleg should be brought in just enough to make the three tracks required, and only forelegs should cross.

Shoulder-in, leg-yielding and the counter-lead at the canter are the only movements in which the horse is required to be bent AWAY FROM THE DIRECTION OF MOVEMENT.

113

STARTING THE SHOULDER-IN

The most common fault is to bring the forehand in too far. When performed 'along the wall' a bend of about 30° from the direction of movement is all that is recommended by the International Rules.

I will instance the right shoulder-in, and that will again require us to have our horse on the right rein. The best place to introduce your horse to the right shoulder-in is immediately after you have ridden around a right-hand corner leading into the long side of the arena.

As we ride around this corner to the right, using the usual body-bending aids, our left leg will be drawn-back and our right **inside** leg will be at or near the girth. Our right rein will be shorter than the left and both reins will be — as always — in contact with the bit.

If we use these aids when coming around the corner and our horse responds correctly, we will have him bent to his right with the left rein touching the outer side of the neck and the right rein clear of the inner side of the neck.

We will find that riding the corner correctly will not only bend the horse as required for the right shoulder-in, but it will also place the rider's legs and hands in the positions they should maintain throughout the shoulder-in movement.

Both horse and rider will now be ready — placed or 'positioned' — for the right shoulder-in.

SHOULDER-IN: THE EXERCISE

Instead of straightening the horse and continuing along the track after the right-hand corner, we should ask our horse to continue on with the part-circle started in the corner — as if we were thinking of riding across the arena on a diagonal line.

As the horse's forefeet step in from the track as if to cross the arena, we then act as though we have just changed our mind about crossing the arena.

Remember, we still have the horse bent around our inside [right] leg, but we should now aim to check his forward movement and convert it to a lateral movement to the left while still maintaining the bend to the right on the horse's neck and body.

We ask him to yield his forehand away from our inside leg — as he has learnt in leg-yielding.

To get him to do this our inside leg will have to increase its lateral demand to produce the shoulder-in. Both reins should gently check the forward movement, but the rider should change the type of contact with the outer rein so as to *invite the horse to 'take' with that outside rein.*

If you have followed Chapter 9 "Control of the Head and Neck", the horse will know what is wanted of him and will 'take' with the outside rein. *We* will KEEP — or maintain — a springy inviting left hand.

When riding a shoulder-in, the inside rein [the right rein in this case] should be well clear of the horse's neck. The lateral movement of the forelegs has to be *the result of the lateral effect of our inside leg.*

Let me repeat: the reins lightly check the forward movement: then the lateral effect of our inside leg which he has learnt in leg-yielding, diverts the horse's impulsion to the left. Our *outside* leg, the left, still drawn-back from rounding the corner, bends the horse's body and keeps the hind legs stepping straight forward along the track. The horse 'taking' with the outside rein also helps to maintain the required bend in his body.

What happens next depends entirely upon the horse's reactions and the rider's skill in dealing with them. From this point on, it is for the rider to encourage his horse INSTANTLY in any tendency to do as is wanted — or, alternatively to gently discourage any tendency to do other than what is wanted.

As ever, our aim should be to make the lesson as easy as we can for the horse to learn; we have him bent when riding through the corner and our aids then suggest that he continues — so bent — along the side of the arena.

Both legs, in addition to their lateral effects, should still continue to drive the horse forward [as set out in Ch. 7]. This is most important, so I will repeat:

"NO LATERAL EFFECT PRODUCED BY EITHER ONE LEG SHOULD EVER REDUCE THE FOR-WARD DEMAND OF BOTH LEGS."

The lateral movement should be obtained by the inside leg; the inside rein must remain clear of the horse's neck.

When the shoulder-in is correctly executed, the hind feet will continue to step along the track at the side of the arena with the forefeet just inside that track [see Fig. 35]. A big bend on the horse's body is not required: it should be limited to some 30° — and of course we do not ask for the full bend at first.

The hind legs must not cross each other: if they do, it means either the rider has taken the forelegs in too far or that the horse has not bent his body as required.

It should be explained here that the wording of the rule dealing with the Shoulder-in [Article 411.7(B)] clashes with the diagram on page 32 of the same Rule Book. The diagram clearly shows the hind legs remaining in the track as at an ordinary move-forward pace.

The horse's inside hind leg should pass, but *not cross* in front of, the outside hind leg.

While remaining upright, the rider should press forward and down with his inside seat-bone [see Ch. 22 'The Ultimate Aids'].

In a correct shoulder-in, the horse's feet move on three tracks:

one . . . outside hind
two . . . inside hind and outside fore
three . . . inside fore.

Fig. 35
LEFT SHOULDER-IN: THE EXERCISE
Mrs Erica Taylor on her stallion "Crown Law". The slight bend of the spine should bring the forelegs in to the left — slightly. Correctly done, as shown, the hinds should remain in the track and step forward without any tendency to cross. The slight bend of the spine should bring the forelegs in to the left a LITTLE without affecting the forward stepping of the hinds.
When correctly executed the horse should move on three tracks, the inside hind moving on the same track as the outside fore. Erica's horses always look happy and attentive.

☆   ☆   ☆

"DON'T HURRY"

On no account rush or hurry these early lateral exercises. They are a means to an end and lead to more difficult movements later on. The lateral effect of a rider's inside leg is not usually obvious to an onlooker, but these exercises ensure that the horse fully understands its requirements and responds to it when asked. The exercises also tend to get the horse to engage his hocks further under his body.

DON'T HURRY. That 'silly leg-yielding' makes the shoulder-in simpler for the horse; and the shoulder-in, in its turn, leads up to the other more difficult movements we have in mind.

Once we can easily get a shoulder-in with the side or wall of the arena helping to keep the horse on the required line, we should then begin to practise it when riding up the centre line. It should be practised at both the walk and trot — but not at a canter.

116

END EACH OF THESE EXERCISES WITH FREE FORWARD
MOVEMENT.

All this part of our horse's schooling should finish with the continuation of
the quarter circle started when rounding the corner.

**Keep in mind that all lateral exercises as well as the rein-back should
always be terminated by free forward movement ... ALWAYS.
We have to be sure we do not let our horse get the impression that
moving sideways is more important than forward movement.**

To reward his horse after such a period of lateral concentration, the late
Capt. J.J. Pearce would 'set him alight' and hand-gallop the arena. He considered
this relaxing and beneficial to both horse and rider.

Fig. 36
Jacqui Cotton introduces her "Princeton"
to lateral exercises . . .

"I don't think it went like that"

TO SUM UP: SHOULDER-IN

The shoulder-in requires the horse to bend his body in answer to the lateral effects of both the inside and outside leg aids when applied simultaneously. The outside leg should be drawn-back to maintain the bend on the horse's body.

The lateral effect of the inside leg must predominate.

When beginning the shoulder-in, we recommend you ride around a corner on to the long side of the arena. This 'positions' both horse and rider for the exercise. The horse is then required to take one step in — as if he were to cross the arena.

The shoulder-in is started by the rider diverting the horse's forward steps by strengthening the lateral effect of the inside leg and by the horse 'taking' with the outside rein, while the outside leg is drawn-back to keep the hind feet stepping straight to their front.

Correctly executed, the horse's hind feet will continue along the track as at a normal walk [or trot].

The bend of the horse's body, head to tail, should be only about 30°, and should result in the horse moving on three tracks.

In both leg-yielding and shoulder-in the horse is required to be bent AWAY from the direction of movement.

As with all lateral work, leg-yielding and shoulder-in should be terminated by free forward movement.

118

CHAPTER 20

TRAVERS, RENVERS AND HALF-PASS

We begin with travers [head to wall];
Introducing travers;
Introducing renvers [tail to wall];
The half-pass.

TRAVERS, RENVERS AND HALF-PASS

The three lateral exercises, travers, renvers and half-pass should be introduced in that order and after leg-yielding and shoulder-in.

In leg-yielding and shoulder-in we required our horse to bend *away* from the direction of movement, and we should note that except for the contra-lead [see Ch. 16] they are the only exercises in which the horse is required to be so bent.

In each of these next movements, travers, renvers and half-pass, the horse is required to flex and bend TOWARDS the direction of movement.

As ever, the rider should be gentle, light and encouraging. He must encourage his horse's tendency to do as is wanted and gently persist with his aids if his horse tends to do other than what is wanted.

WE BEGIN WITH TRAVERS [HEAD TO WALL]

Once again let us start off on the right rein and, as with the shoulder-in, from the corner preceeding the long side of the arena. Doing so will again position both horse and rider — but this time we begin, but the hind feet do not quite complete, the riding through the corner.

As his forefeet meet the track and before his hind feet have reached it: while the horse still has his body bent to the right: our reins and our driving aids should keep the forefeet in the track, our already drawn-back leg should increase its lateral effect and move the hindquarters to the right, while our inside leg, assisted by the reins, keeps the bend he already has on his body.

> *Impulsion, as always, must be maintained by the riders driving aids —*
> *legs and seat.*

We must be sure that both horse and rider KEEP the outside rein — and I will repeat, "the forward driving leg effects must *never* be lessened by any lateral demands made by our legs".

The side to which the horse should be bent — the right in this case — is the 'inside'.

119

INTRODUCING TRAVERS

We now have our horse placed, or 'positioned'. Our legs and seat maintain impulsion and the bend on the horse's body; and our outside leg now takes on **the additional task of moving the quarters somewhat sideways along the inside of the track.**

The forehand has to be kept in the track while the quarters move along the inside of the track — and the bend on our horse's body will allow for this.

The horse will be bent to his right, the side to which he is to move, in this instance [see Fig. 37].

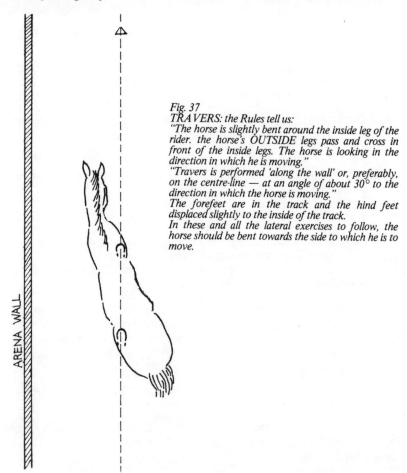

Fig. 37
TRAVERS: the Rules tell us:
"The horse is slightly bent around the inside leg of the rider. the horse's OUTSIDE legs pass and cross in front of the inside legs. The horse is looking in the direction in which he is moving."
"Travers is performed 'along the wall' or, preferably, on the centre-line — at an angle of about 30° to the direction in which the horse is moving."
The forefeet are in the track and the hind feet displaced slightly to the inside of the track.
In these and all the lateral exercises to follow, the horse should be bent towards the side to which he is to move.

ARENA WALL

As always, we should not ask for a big bend at first; 30° will be the limit asked for eventually, but at first we should be content to obtain a lesser degree. Getting our horse to 'take' with the outside rein will help keep his head and neck to the right, while our legs will maintain the bend of his body, the lateral movement of his hind legs — and impulsion.

Well before this time the rider should have begun the use of seat-bone pressures — and the seat pressures will eventually take the place of the leg aids. To *assist the horse* the rider should press forward and down on his right seat-bone and his right stirrup — but not lean his body [see Ch. 22 'The Ultimate Aids'].

The aids used should be as light as possible and it is for the rider to feel, through his seat, for the slightest tendency on the part of the horse to do as we want — and then we must let him know that we are pleased with him. Murmur to him and reward by "End of Lesson" for a while.

With all these exercises, the rider must REPEATEDLY check himself for stiffness. "Down the weight" and "Upright the body"; and he should see, too, that the horse occasionally 'tastes the bit'. Keep him relaxed and check that you, yourself, remain relaxed.

So much for Travers: now for Renvers.

INTRODUCING RENVERS [TAIL TO WALL]

The Rule Book lists Renvers as: "The inverse movement in relation to Travers" [I always think of renvers as the exercise in which the horse is reversed — and puts his reverse — or rear — end in the track].

In travers it is the hindquarters that have to be kept to the inside of the track. In renvers, it is the forehand that has to be brought to the inside of the track; and there is nothing to be gained from starting renvers immediately after rounding a corner [see Fig. 38].

> *The important difference between each of these exercises and the shoulder-in lies in the bend required of the horse: AWAY from the direction of movement in leg-yielding and shoulder-in — and TOWARDS the direction of movement in all these later and more advanced lateral exercises.*

Renvers will pose no problem for a horse and rider at home with travers.

121

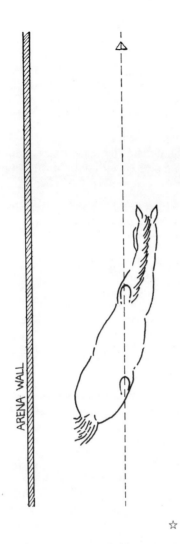

ARENA WALL

Fig. 38 A
RENVERS: the Rules tell us:
"Renvers is the inverse movement in relation to travers, with the tail instead of the head to the wall. Otherwise, the same principles and conditions are applicable as at the travers."
The forefeet are displaced slightly to the inside of the track, while the hind feet step along in the track.

☆   ☆   ☆

I propose to say little more about the aids to be used for these more advanced lateral movements, for it should not be necessary for a rider of this standard to learn them from the written word.

The points I will stress are:

. . . first, have a clear picture in your mind of what is to be asked of the horse; and

. . . then, be most careful to avoid the use of force — heavy aids.

The use of force is not only unnecessary but it defeats its own end: the horse loses calmness; and as I so often repeat *calmness is essential when introducing any lesson.*

122

☆   ☆   ☆

Practise both travers and renvers along the wall at first if you have the use of an indoor school: the wall helps the horse to grasp the idea of what is wanted. Later, ask for them both along the centre-line where they are sometimes asked for in competition.

Fig. 38B
RENVERS RIGHT — the exercise. In the test shown [Intermediate No. 1, Australian Dressage Championships] the rider is required to ride 'Renvers Right' along the centre-line from "X" after having just completed an 8m circle to the right at that marker.
The circle has the horse bent to the right and the illustration shows Mrs Erica Taylor is positioning "Crown Prince" along the centre-line on which she has to ride 'Renvers Right'. The horse is slightly bent to the right, and the outside legs pass and cross in front of the inside legs.

We should keep these and all other lateral lessons short; be instant with your encouragements when your horse shows the slightest tendency to do as you ask.

Sometime later in his training we will ask him to move on circles with his hindquarters displaced, or bent, to the inside of the circle — travers on a circle — and this in its turn will lead to pirouettes [the pirouette, I note, is not listed as a lateral exercise].

Again I remind you . . . terminate all lateral movements by riding your horse forward. We have to be sure we keep our horse ready to move forward. Every now and again send him off into something in the nature of a gallop after these lateral exercises; let him forget his lessons for a while.

With travers and renvers mastered, horse and rider should now be ready for the half-pass.

☆   ☆   ☆

123

THE HALF-PASS

The half-pass is little more than a variation of the travers and is usually executed diagonally across the arena instead of along the side or wall. I will instance a right half-pass [see Fig. 39].

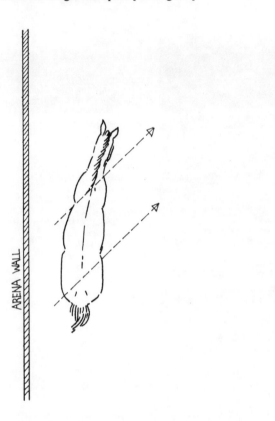

Fig. 39

THE HALF-PASS

This is a variation of travers, executed on the diagonal instead of along the wall.
The forehand should be slightly in advance of the quarters and the horse slightly bent around the rider's inside leg. The outside legs should pass and cross in front of the inside legs.
The maintenance of impulsion is most important and the rhythm and balance should be maintained.
The whole of the horse's body should be SLIGHTLY bent around the inside leg of the rider.
The rider: weight "down", head and eyes "up".

For the right half-pass we will first need to put our horse on the right rein in the manege. Let us ride around the corner on to the long side and then ask our horse to start to cross the arena on a diagonal line to his right. His body should be

124

kept nearly parallel with the side of the school — but only 'nearly' parallel, for his forehand should slightly precede his quarters.

The horse is required to be bent and look in the direction in which he is moving, and his outside legs should pass and cross in front of the inside legs. [Remember, 'inside' is the side to which he should be bent, to the right in a half-pass to the right.]

In the half-pass across the arena the horse should be slightly bent around the inside leg of the rider. The forehand should be a little in front of the hind-quarters, the horse should be slightly bent into the direction of movement and **the rider should look up and in the direction of movement.**

The rider should assist his horse by increasing the weight on his inside seat-bone and stirrup [see Ch. 22]. His outside leg, slightly drawn-back, is responsible for the sideways movement; it should influence the horse to place his foot further under his body and away from its pressure.

The horse must show a definite impulsion and if he is correctly bent, his outside legs will cross in front of his inside legs [see Fig. 40], and the inside hind leg will step well under his body. This inducing the horse to bring the inside hind 'leg well under the body is one of the objectives of these lateral exercises.

Fig. 40
HALF PASS TO THE LEFT: Mrs E. Taylor on her "Crown Prince" in a training session. The horse — at a walk — is well bent into the direction of movement with the outside legs crossing in front of the inside legs. Erica's comment when shown the picture was: "I should have made more weight on the inside seat-bone and heel!"

125

A very important point is that both horse and rider should 'keep' the outside rein. Rhythm, balance and impulsion should be maintained throughout the exercise — which may be asked for at the walk, trot or canter.

As with all new exercises, ask for only a few paces at first — and then reward your horse by "End of Lesson" and ride him straight to his front.

TO SUM UP

In these and all movements other than leg-yielding, shoulder-in and counter-canter, the horse is required to be bent into the direction of movement.

In travers the horse is required to move along the side of the arena bent into the direction of movement, with his quarters moving along the inside of the track.

Travers is a valuable exercise, much used to introduce more difficult exercises such as the pirouette.

Renvers is a similar movement along the wall or side, but with the quarters remaining on the track and the forehand on the inside of the track.

The half-pass is little more than a travers in a different direction, usually diagonally across the arena.

To be able to get the horse to 'take' with the outside rein is ESSENTIAL in all advanced work. The horse should 'take' into the required direction whenever asked and the rider should 'keep' the outside rein.

The use of any force should be avoided: use only light aids. Be gentle and encouraging whenever opportunity offers; try to get the horse to taste the bit occasionally.

Maintaining impulsion is of the greatest importance, and the horse should be ridden forward at the end of each exercise.

The paces should be regular and free.

CHAPTER 21

THE PIROUETTE AND HALF-PIROUETTE

The pirouette — the horse is required to turn a complete
circle by pivoting around his inside hind foot;
Backward or outward movement not permitted;
"Ride the horse forward" — Franz Mairinger;
Sequence of footfalls must be maintained.

THE PIROUETTE

F.E.I. Rule 412 tells us: "A pirouette is a circle executed on two tracks, with a radius equal to the length of the horse, the forehand moving around the haunches".

Pirouettes and half-pirouettes are only carried out at the walk or canter, and the exact rhythm and sequence of footfalls as well as a light contact, hand and leg, *must be maintained.*

The horse's forefeet and his outside hind foot are required to move around his inside hind foot, which forms the pivot and which should be picked up and returned to the same spot or only slightly in front of it, each time it leaves the ground.

At whatever pace the pirouettes or half-pirouettes are executed, the horse is slightly bent to the direction in which he is turning and should remain "on the bit".

A properly executed pirouette is a very advanced movement and my purpose in detailing it here is to advise the student to be sure he aims only to practise the movements that LEAD to a pirouette at first. Make haste slowly.

It is interesting to note that the pirouette is not listed as a lateral movement, as only three legs move to the side.

INTRODUCING THE PIROUETTE

Fig. 41 is designed to show how, when riding an advanced horse on a circle, the track of the hind feet can be kept to the inside of the track of the forefeet by using much the same aids as for travers. We require 'travers right' while riding on a right-hand circle, and 'travers left' on a left-hand circle.

The circles or part-circles should be quite large at first — but whatever the size of the circle traced by the forefeet, the track of the hind feet should be smaller. This will be due to the bend we place on the body of our horse when riding travers.

127

As training and understanding progress, smaller and smaller circles are asked of the horse, until eventually the inside hind foot is picked up and replaced in the same or almost the same spot [see Fig. 42], and the other three legs move around it. And remember — the *exact rhythm and sequence of footfalls as well as a light contact, hands and legs, must be maintained.*

In short, the horse must remain 'On the bit'.

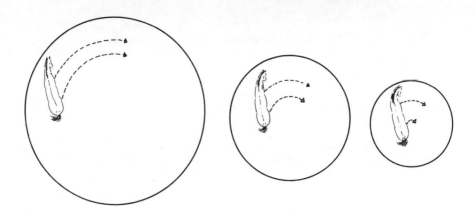

Fig. 41

THE PIROUETTE AND HALF-PIROUETTE

The half-pirouette is always asked for before the full pirouette.
The large circle shows how the horse is introduced to the circle with the hindquarters in, by asking for a travers movement — the right in this case. The inside hind leg moves on a smaller circle than the other three legs.
The size of the circles is gradually reduced, as shown, until eventually the inside hind leg is picked up and put down again on the same spot, and the other legs move around it.

Figs 42A & 42B
THE HALF PIROUETTE TO THE LEFT, FROM THE WALK
A — Mrs Erica Taylor on "Crown Prince" begins a half-pirouette to the left. The off-hind and the two fore legs move around the inside hind leg.
B — The half-pirouette almost completed with the inside hind about to be replaced on the spot from which it was raised.

ALL STEPS MUST BE FORWARD AND IN
THE DIRECTION OF THE PIROUETTE

The aim is to make the circles, with hindquarters in, smaller and smaller until eventually the inside hind leg is picked up and put down on the same spot. But before we think of asking for this — *the ultimate* — we repeatedly ask for circles or part-circles with the quarters in and with the inside hind leg making a small to a very small circle.

We should aim to give our horse the *idea* of what is wanted of him at first: a step or two of the pirouette and then forward and relax. We should not ask for a full pirouette or even a half-pirouette at first. Ask only for a quarter pirouette or even less — and at a walk.

A step to the rear, no matter how small, clearly shows that the rider has permitted his horse to lose impulsion. He is no longer 'on the bit'. The horse has to be RIDDEN FORWARD into this, and all other movements, at this more advanced stage of his schooling [see Ch. 11 "On the Bit"].

Again, it is most important that the rider invites the horse to 'take' with the outside rein [see Ch. 9].

"RIDE THE HORSE FORWARD": FRANZ MAIRINGER

The only way to keep our horse up to the bit is for the rider to demand forward movement *at any step* of this movement — at *any* step. We should repeatedly ride the horse forward after only two or three steps of the movement: this keeps him attentive to the forward effects of our forward-driving aids. If you continually ask for a forward tendency and never enforce the forward steps, the horse will soon come to ignore your forward demand. The lateral effects will dominate his mind.

Repeatedly .. we must ride the horse forward after only one or two steps of the turn. He has to pick up his inside hind foot as though to go forward, and not until he has picked it up should he know if he is to be asked to put it down in the same place — or step forward.

The only way to be sure he will pick that inside foot up is to *ride him forward repeatedly in his schooling.* He has to go forward and up to the bit to feel there for what the bit has to tell him. He must be kept EXPECTING AND READY to be driven forward at each and every step.

Although that inside hind foot is not permitted to move back or to the outside, a trifling forward movement is not frowned upon.

Be firm in your demand for an immediate and ready response to the forward effects of the legs, but don't be rough or harsh if he is slow off the mark. Let him find that rewards will always follow immediate obedience. "That will profit you", "End of Lesson", and all that.

130

A horse that has reached pirouettes has proved himself to be a willing horse. Encouraging his tendencies to do as is wanted of him will prove to be much more effective than anything in the nature of punishment.

THE IMPORTANCE OF IMPULSION

Although the lateral effects of hand and leg might seem to predominate in this circling with the hindquarters kept to the inside of the circle, *in actuality the forward drive of the rider's legs and seat — the impulsion — must always predominate and our horse respond to LIGHT driving aids.*

JUDGING THE PIROUETTE

Rule 412.6 gives this instruction to judges and competitors:

> "The quality of the pirouettes or half-pirouettes is judged according to the suppleness, lightness, cadence and regularity, and to the precision and smoothness of the transitions; pirouettes and half-pirouettes at the canter also according to the balance, the elevation and the number of strides [at pirouettes 6-8; at half-pirouettes 3-4 are desirable]".

TO SUM UP

In a pirouette or part-pirouette the horse is required to pivot around his inside hind leg with the other three legs moving forward and around that pivot.

The inside hind foot has to be picked up and returned to the same spot with the same rhythm and sequence of steps as if he were being ridden straight forward.

The four-steps of a walk or the three-steps of the canter must be maintained throughout the movement and the horse flexed to the direction in which he is to turn.

On no account may the pivoting foot step backward or outward in the slightest degree — but a small forward movement should not be penalised.

The pirouette and all part-pirouettes should result from smaller and smaller circles ridden with the hindquarters kept to the inside, until eventually the small circle described by the inside hind becomes 'on the spot'.

Repeatedly 'ride the horse forward' during these exercises; he has to be kept ready and expecting to move forward at any step — ALWAYS.

A pirouette is a very advanced movement and should only be started under the eye of a competent instructor.

Plenty of variety is needed to keep a horse interested in what he is doing — occasionally give him a change of ground and of scenery, and a pleasant ride as a 'that will profit you' reward.

CHAPTER 22

THE ULTIMATE AIDS

Importance of lightness and of 'feel'
End-goal of lightness of hand;
Substituting 'seat' for 'legs';
"The horse's shoulders should remain parallel to . . .";
"The horse's hips should remain parallel to . . .";
Rider's weight as an aid.

I find myself asking the question as I write on: "For whom am I writing this book?"

There can be no doubt about the answer — it is for the young and aspiring rider I write: and certainly not for those approaching 'high school' standards.

Nevertheless I now propose to include at least one chapter that may be of help to any rider with eyes set in that direction. In addition to setting out some of my ideas of what is right, I want, too, to say something of a practice that I know is definitely NOT RIGHT: the substitution *of excessive and unsightly body movement* for the forward-driving seat and leg aids.

EXCESSIVE BODY AIDS

Watching these riders, it seems their horses accept the incessant banging of ribs and the swinging bodies as meaning only: "Don't stop yet . . . don't stop yet". Certainly their horses show no inclination to increase impulsion or pace.

Throughout schooling, one of our first aims should be to get immediate responses to our forward-driving leg aids: aids so light that they are hardly visible. Everything in dressage hinges on our ability to get our horse responsive to light forward-driving aids — so I am adding this chapter on "The Ultimate Aids" in the hope that it will inspire riders to tackle this problem, if it is one they are facing. I want to give some insight as to the POSSIBLE delicacy of aids used as we ride into first class dressage.

Can I get you to 'raise your sights' and give that horse of yours an occasional smart tap with the whip to make him attend to you — if he is not doing so? It is not a matter of being cruel or harsh; indeed you will be doing him a kindness by showing him how he can avoid having his ribs incessantly thumped or how he can stop you swinging your body about the way you do. If you find it necessary to use your spurs or whip sharply, be sure you see that he responds instantly — so that you do not need to repeat it.

Our ultimate aim in dressage should be to educate our horse to do anything we want in answer to aids so small, so light, that an onlooker will be unable to see any aids being used. [See Fig. 43.]

Fig. 43
"THE ULTIMATE" to most dressage riders —
At Wembley, 1973, Fr Liselott Linsenhoff on "Piaff". The rider looks well up and in the direction of movement. The horse, with mouth softly 'on the bit' is fully intent on his rider's aids. He moves with great impulsion — and appears to enjoy demonstrating his understanding of his rider.
[Courtesy of and splendidly photographed by Clive Hiles of London.]

Once again I have to stress the importance of light leg aids, for which we aim to substitute changes in our seat pressures . . . but if we have failed to get our horse light to the legs, there is little hope of our getting responses to the seat-bone movements and changes.

☆   ☆   ☆

THE ULTIMATE IN REIN AIDS
"The horse's shoulders should remain parallel with the rider's shoulders . . ."

I quote the late Mr Franz Mairinger.

"THE HORSE'S SHOULDERS SHOULD REMAIN PARALLEL WITH HIS RIDER'S SHOULDERS . . ."

When horse and rider are ready for this stage of training, all we need to do with our reins when we wish to change direction is to move our hands by turning our shoulders a few degrees towards the required direction *while keeping our arms and hands still in relation to our shoulders.*

The rider merely 'looks in the direction in which he wishes to move'; and he should do this, not by turning his head only but by turning head, shoulders and arms: his whole upper body: a few degrees.

This will not only move both hands towards the side to which he wishes his horse to move, but it also increases the contact on the inside rein, which should tend to become resistant, while tending to decrease the contact — or feel — on the outside rein which should invite the horse to 'take rein'.

Shoulders, arms and hands should maintain their relative position one to the other and the movement of the shoulders should be such that an onlooker will find it difficult to see any movement or change in the position of the rider's hands.

HOW IT WORKS

You can demonstrate to yourself how this turning of the shoulders operates by trying it right now while sitting in your chair. Sit yourself near a table and place your hands in a riding position — and about an inch [2 cm] from the edge of the table. Now turn your head and shoulders a few degrees to your right.

Note the lateral movement of both hands, the small backward movement of the inside hand and the equal forward movement of the outside hand.

The great value of the above quotation lies in the so-small movement it recommends and the fact that our *hands do not move* in relation to our arms and shoulders, although our fingers still make their delicate adjustments.

The size of any circle or other movement to be ridden will determine the degree of turn the rider should make with his shoulders and upper part of his body. The movement of our hands — the result of the movement of our shoulders — will require **the horse to bend his forehand and move his shoulders to exactly the same degree.**

In other words the horse is required, through the reins, to keep his shoulders parallel to the rider's shoulders.

He is actually only answering the usual rein-aids for a change of direction. The outside hand invites the horse to 'take' and the inside hand invites him to 'give'; the rider's fingers maintain their independence and keep contact.

134

THE ULTIMATE IN "DRIVING" AIDS
" . . . and the horse's hips should remain parallel with the
rider's hips"   — Franz Mairinger

". . . THE HORSE'S HIPS SHOULD REMAIN
PARALELL WITH HIS RIDER'S HIPS . . ."

This requirement is not so simple for the horse to understand, and teaching
him to keep his hips parallel to the rider's hips requires introductory exercises.

Long before we have reached this stage we will have taught our horse the
lateral aids that require him to bend his spine to the right or left. For instance,
when making a circle to the right we have used our drawn-back outside leg, and
with the inside leg remaining on or near the girth we have taught him to bend his
body to the right [see Ch. 10] and he clearly understands and responds freely to our
leg aids both lateral and forward-driving.

Now we aim to substitute our seat-bone pressures for the leg aids when
requiring a body-bend and increased impulsion. At first we will continue to use our
legs to produce the bend of the spine, and at the same time as we turn our
shoulders we should push our *inside seat-bone forward and down.*

At first we may need to give our inside seat-bone a definite push forward
and down, strong enough to draw the horse's attention to it. With repetition he will
come to associate this seat-movement with the demands of our legs, and it is then
for the rider to progressively diminish the strength of his ordinary leg aids until
eventually the horse responds to the changes of seat pressures alone.

As our horse comes to notice and respond to the — at first — quite marked
seat-bone aids, they, too, should become lighter and lighter until *the horse learns to
keep his hips parallel to his rider's hips when he feels his rider move his inside seat-
bone forward and down.* [The seat-bone forms — of course — part of our hips, our
pelvis.]

Remember, when changing direction the horse's hind legs have to move in
a slightly different direction from his fronts. This taking our inside hip-bone
forward and seeing that he does the same, will ensure the necessary bend in our
horse's back — when he understands it.

> *Briefly: at first the leg-aids will precede the seat-aids. Next, both leg
> and seat aids are used simultaneously. Then we let our leg aids become
> lighter and lighter until the horse acts on the movement of the seat
> alone.*

Occasionally a lazy horse will need a reminder from the legs just as in his
early education he occasionally needed a sharper reminder from heel or whip.
But . . . what chance will we have of getting him to attend to these so much less
obvious seat pressures if we have been unable to obtain an immediate response to
our light leg aids?

135

THE HORSE'S READINESS TO MOVE FORWARD AT THE SLIGHTEST INDICATION OF THE DRIVING AIDS MUST PREDOMINATE FROM THE FIRST STAGE OF TRAINING TO THE LAST.

RIDER'S WEIGHT AS AN AID

During the latter stages of the horse's training, the rider's weight also becomes an aid: always when changing direction the rider should add a little weight on to his inside stirrup. As schooling progresses, this trifling increase of weight on the inside stirrup becomes more and more important. *What's more, just pushing forward and down with our inside seat-bone will increase the weight on the inside stirrup.*

If you want to prove the lateral effect of adding a little weight to the inside seat-bone, just try — as I did many years ago — the effect of putting a little extra weight on to one seat-bone or the other, when riding a bicycle.

Ride on a slight downward slope, and as you are gently coasting along, try putting some weight on one side of the saddle. Keep your body upright, and press down a little on the right seat-bone.

You will find the bicycle immediately moves to that side.

Where does the extra weight come from when you press down on one seat-bone? From the OTHER seat-bone: as it does when you are on a bicycle.

Remember, you will meet no resistance from a bicycle; and when the horse is brought to the same stage of non-resistance, he too will answer by changing direction if you are consistent.

ADDING TO THE WEIGHT IN THE STIRRUP

Now let's see what other changes should occur when we push one seat-bone forward and down when riding a horse.

When the rider pushes one seat-bone forward and down the top of his thigh-bone goes forward with it.

It is most important, when using our seat as an aid, that the forward movement of the *top* of the thigh-bone, which is joined to the seat-bone, does not move the lower end of the thigh-bone — the knee — forward.

> *If you do not allow the knee to move forward, then it is compelled to move downward — and in doing so, it increases the weight on the stirrup under the knee.*

Let me detail again what happens. When a seat-bone is moved forward, the top of the thigh-bone moves forward a fraction with it, and so the thigh-bone becomes a little more perpendicular. As the top of the thigh is not allowed to lift and the knee is not permitted to move forward, then the knee and all that is below it must drop a trifle.

136

You can check the mechanics of this seat and heel movement, too, as you set on a chair. The chair needs to be high enough to have the bend of your knee similar to that when in the saddle.

☆   ☆   ☆

The use of the rider's seat and body-weight as aids belongs to more advanced dressage. Although I have referred to them from time to time, I have left this explanation of the mechanics of their employment until now, as:

> FIRST, the horse has to be taught to answer the forward-drive of the legs;
> THEN, when that is clearly understood, we introduce our horse to body-bending exercises.
> THEN, AND ONLY THEN, we start to introduce the final — the ultimate — aids of seat and weight placement.

Even if you have no intention of going on to Advanced Dressage, I feel you should know something of the demands likely to be made of your horse at that standard.

Our horse MUST respond to the lightest aids . . . and my purpose in appending this chapter on "The Ultimate Aids" is to let my readers know just how light to the aids the horse *can* be brought to be.

Do not tolerate disobedience or half-hearted obedience to the legs: our horse has to be as nice to us as we are prepared to be to him.

TO SUM UP

It is most important for a rider to realise that if he cannot bring his horse to answer very light leg aids there is little likelihood of getting him to respond to even lighter seat-aids.

Instant obedience to the lightest leg aid is a first essential. The horse must obey: you must discipline him if necessary once he understands the aid.

The horse's shoulders should remain parallel to the rider's shoulders; the rider moves shoulders-arms-hands instead of just hands; the fingers still make their own delicate adjustments.

The horse's hips should remain parallel to the rider's hips.

Having taught the horse to bend his spine in answer to leg aids, the rider begins to use his inside seat-bone at the same time as he uses the leg-aids.

Use of the seat-bone is pronounced **at first** but as the horse comes to notice it the leg effect is decreased, until he acts on the influence of the seat-bone alone.

When turning or moving to one side, weight added to the inside stirrup will help the horse to move that way. Seat-bone pressures will produce the weight movement desired, when correctly done.

Our ultimate aim is to have our horse execute the most difficult movements in response to aids that are invisible.

NOTHING IN THE NATURE OF PRONOUNCED OR JERKY BODY-MOVEMENT IS TOLERATED IN THE RIDER.

CHAPTER 23

THE FLYING CHANGE

Importance of the hind leg;
The period of suspension;
PREP .. AR .. ATION;
Timing most important;
Introducing the flying change;
Don't forget the counter-canter;
Flying changes in series.

IMPORTANCE OF THE HIND LEG

Simple changes of leg at the canter have been dealt with in Chapter 17 of 'HORSE CONTROL — THE YOUNG HORSE'. The flying change of leg is an advanced movement and I don't propose to say much about it here although a few· facts might be of interest to those now approaching this standard.

F.E.I. Rules deal with both simple and flying changes as follows:

Article 405[6] — Simple Change of Leg at Canter
"This is a change of leg where the horse is brought back into·walk and, after two or at the most three steps, is restarted into a canter with the other leg leading."

Article 405[7] — Flying Change of Leg in the Air
"This change of leg is executed in close connection with the suspension which follows each stride of the canter. Flying changes of leg can also be executed in series, for instance at every 4th, 3rd, 2nd or at every stride. The horse, even in the series, remains light, calm and straight with lively impulsion, maintaining the same rhythm and balance throughout the series concerned. In order not to restrict or restrain the lightness and fluency of the flying changes of leg in series, the degree of collection should be slightly less than otherwise at collected canter."

Be sure you study Chapter 22, "The Ultimate Aids", before you begin to ask for a flying change.

THE PERIOD OF SUSPENSION

You will know that a canter is a pace of three-time. If the horse is to lead with his off-fore, his footfalls will run: [1] near hind; [2] left diagonal; [3] off-fore — leading. If he is to lead with the near-fore, his footfalls will run: [1] off-hind; [2] right diagonal; then [3] near-fore leading.

139

In each case, these footfalls will be followed by a short period of suspension during which all four feet will be off the ground.

After each period of suspension it is the hind leg that the horse places on the ground first which determines the leg that will come to the ground last — which leg "leads".

To get the horse to change the leading fore-leg, we have to be able to get him to change the hind legs during the period of suspension when all four legs are off the ground.

As with every other exercise the maintenance of impulsion is a primary consideration.

PREP . . AR . . ATION

No thought should be given to the flying change until we have our horse light to all the aids and 'on the bit'.

He should be at home with lateral exercises and seat-aids, and be easily put into a trot or canter on any nominated leg from the halt or walk.

He should be able to strike off on either the correct leg or the counter-lead on quite small circles when asked. *The counter-canter is a most important part of the preparation.*

Impulsion and willing obedience to the driving aids are essential, for the rider's legs and seat will command the flying change.

TIMING IS MOST IMPORTANT

I must stress the importance of asking for the flying change at precisely the right moment, which is: " . . . the moment the horse is about to lift his leading forefoot off the ground." That is, a moment before the period of suspension, as mentioned in the rules.

The rider needs to develop — and use — his sense of 'feel' to judge the correct timing to make the demand for the change. As he canters around his arena, he must sit down in his saddle and FEEL THERE for the movement of that leading leg. The rider should note to himself, 'now', 'now', 'now' . . . **each time the leading leg is about to be raised.**

"Look up and feel down", "down the weight": and note the timing until you are sure you can feel the exact moment to ask for the change. Check that you, yourself, are relaxed at all times. Having your weight down to feel for the footfalls should ensure you are relaxed.

At the right moment — the moment the leading leg is about to leave the ground — quietly and lightly ask for the change.

It's the old story. First, teach all the exercises leading up to the demand to be made; then, when he is calm and relaxed, place and prepare the horse for the new requirement.

INTRODUCING THE FLYING CHANGE

In my day, when I thought the horse was ready, I would often take the following course [if riding in a manege] to make it easy for both the horse and myself.

At a corner. On the left rein, let us say, canter around the manege with the near-fore leading; then change rein, from 'F' to 'H' across the arena. Each time you arrive at the corner near 'H', still on the near lead, make a simple change of leg there in the corner. This can be practised well before the flying change is to be asked for, and we should finally allow only a single walking pace before asking for the canter on the off lead.

Do this several times and your horse could well start to think as he nears the corner: "Here we go again, another change of lead" — and he won't be surprised when eventually you ask him to make the change without first dropping to a walk.

The corner will change his direction and bring his forehand around, and the reins are hardly needed. No roughness, no pulling or jerking to distract the horse's attention from the leg and seat aids.

The outside leg should be lightly drawn-back and the inside seat-bone should be pushed forward to ask for the flying change.

We should use our hands as lightly as possible in the situation just described, so that the horse is able to give all his attention to our legs and seat. In the beginning, the rider uses the diagonal aids to ask the horse for a change of leg in the air; as the horse progresses in training and becomes thoroughly responsive to the diagonal aids, these can be lessened and lateral aids gradually introduced. Once he has been introduced and properly understands them, the seat aids become most important in the flying change. [See Ch. 22.]

Rewards must be instant when the horse does make the flying change. Canter on for a few strides, then 'End of Lesson', perhaps for the day. I need hardly say the simple changes will first be asked for on both reins — as eventually will the flying changes.

NEXT: ASK FOR THE FLYING CHANGE ELSEWHERE

When our horse is familiar with and well-practised at a flying change in each of the corners, it is time to prepare him for the changes riding figures-of-eight or with other changes of direction.

Start by riding figures-of-eight — or other changes of direction such as a zig-zag course — bring him down to a single walking stride as you did in the corner. Use your reins as lightly as possible and see that your weight is well down in your saddle — and feel for the exact moment to ask for the flying change. Although the outside leg should be drawn-back, remember it is the seat aid that is really important, for later on we will have to ask for changes on a straight line using aids that are not visible.

DON'T NEGLECT THE COUNTER-CANTER

Do not ask for a flying change at every change of direction. Quite often, make the second bend without asking for a change of lead; keep him on the counter-lead occasionally, for it is an exercise he does not like and it makes your request to change on to the correct lead very welcome.

Do not hurry. And do not let your horse become upset or in any way stiff — he still has a long way to go. Above all things, keep him calm so that he will notice and attend to those seat aids.

FLYING CHANGES OF LEG IN SERIES

You will have noted the rule says: "Flying changes of leg can also be executed in series . . ." at every fourth, third, second or at every stride. This means that the horse will be asked to make a flying change on a straight line — eventually at every stride. The horse has to remain: "light, calm and straight, with lively impulsion".

Unlike the rein-back, the flying change comes naturally to all horses. Watch any group of horses cantering loose in a paddock, and notice how even the youngest foal will change legs with a flying change when making changes of direction.

We do not have to 'teach' the flying change; all we have to do is to teach our horse the aids so that he knows WHEN we want him to change leg. The important thing is for the rider not to use aids that will upset either his horse's — or his own — balance or calmness.

When we get to the stage where we can get flying changes on a straight line we are really making progress in our dressage.

Capt. J.J. Pearce would occasionally use this flying change in the corner as just detailed. When his horse made the flying change in each corner without loss of calmness or hurrying, he would ask for it a step or so before reaching the corner — while the horse was still on the straight line. His horse might miss the change the first time of asking, but with a few repeats he had him making the change on the straight line leading to the corner. The horse should be kept straight so that his quarters do not swing out of alignment.

Some riders prefer other means to introduce a horse to the flying change; some use different methods with different horses. I recommend the change in the corner, then the change on the straight line leading to the corner — but on no account start to work on a second method until the preceding exercise is confirmed.

142

IN EVERY METHOD IT IS THE COUNTER-CANTER THAT IS SO IMPORTANT.

Your horse must be thoroughly at home with the requirements of this exercise, and he must obey your requests to canter on what he knows is the 'wrong' leg, well before we think of asking for the flying change.

It is most important that the rider checks that he, himself, remains relaxed. Do all that is possible to keep the horse calm and quiet — and his body straight. No fuss and plenty of praise whenever he tends to do better.

Go back to slower work for a few days if you find your horse becoming upset or rushing his changes, or becoming 'routined'. Keep him interested in his work, one day at school and collected exercises and the next hacking or extended paces. If you are using a double bridle, return to the snaffle frequently.

Many of the horses I schooled were for polo, and I did most of their work in wide open spaces. I included the flying change in their work, not that a flying change is demanded in the game — but to make the pony feel free to change leg when changing direction. I felt it an advantage for the rider to be able to ask for, and obtain, a flying change when he saw a change would be needed. Pat, my wife, often shows films of these ponies making flying changes at very small changes of direction and on the straight. I learnt a lot from dressage.

But . . . it is most difficult to learn these advanced exercises from the written word alone. An instructor — a good one — is strongly recommended . . . and no matter how far a rider progresses, he should take a "refresher" lesson whenever the opportunity presents itself. An instructor has at least one great advantage — *he can see you.*

TO SUM UP

The flying change is an advanced movement and the maintenance of impulsion is the primary consideration.

Careful preparation is needed — and the horse should be positioned where it is easy for him to execute a change of lead in the air.

Keep the horse calm — and straight.

Read again Ch. 17 of "HORSE CONTROL — THE YOUNG HORSE" and all it has to say about the simple change of lead. I am assuming you have read this work, and particularly pp. 161-2.

Reward whenever your horse shows progress.

Remember the ultimate aim is to have your horse execute flying changes — on the straight — using aids through the seat and hands that the onlooker cannot see.

CHAPTER 24

INTRODUCING JUMPING

CAVALETTI — THEIR CONSTRUCTION — AND EARLY JUMPING

Nothing quite so useful;
Instruction on how to make your own cavaletti;
First jumping lessons;
Evolution of show-jumping seat;
Again — PREP .. AR .. ATION.

NOTHING QUITE SO USEFUL

It is doubtful if any set of jumps could be quite so useful in the training of horse and rider as a set of six to twelve cavaletti. [See Figs. 44 to 54.]

A cavaletti consists of a single pole permanently secured at each end to small stands shaped like an "X". The stands will be about 2 feet high, but the pole is lower as it has to be bolted a little off the centre of the stand. This has the advantage that each pole can be set at three different heights by merely turning the cavaletti upside down or on to its side.

It is important that all cavaletti be the same length and similarly constructed so that they can be placed one upon the other to build obstacles easily and quickly, without an assistant.

They are not recommended for high fences: although they can be used to build fences of any height. Versatility is the outstanding feature of the cavaletti. A rider, even when alone, can build all sorts of combinations — singles, double or treble jumps, and can make the jumps as wide as he likes.

Any bush carpenter can make cavaletti — and the following instructions will make their construction even easier.

INSTRUCTIONS FOR MAKING YOUR OWN CAVALETTI

An 8ft. 4in. length of 4in. x 4in. [or 4"x3"] timber will cut into the four end-pieces necessary for one cavaletti. The size recommended is not so much for strength as for the wider platform provided by the larger section when placing one cavaletti upon the other.

Each 8ft. 4in. [or equivalent metric] length of timber has to be cut in exactly the same manner. I stress this, as it may at first seem that the two opposite sides of each cross should be marked and cut the opposite of each other. This is not so. Mark and cut them exactly the same, and they will face 'opposite' when one is turned.

144

The following diagrams will help:

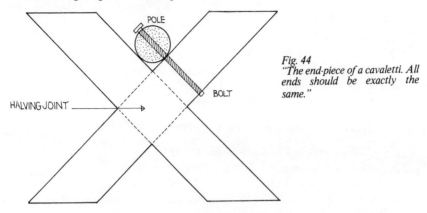

Fig. 44
"The end-piece of a cavaletti. All ends should be exactly the same."

Now to mark the length of timber for cutting:

Fig. 45
"All timber for cutting should be marked in EXACTLY the same manner."

The above is how your piece of timber should look after marking.

Next, turn it over and repeat the markings there.

The pieces when cut have to be crossed at right angles, and it is necessary to use a halving-joint:

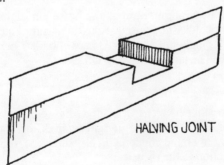

HALVING JOINT

Fig. 46
The halving-joint should be cut at right angles to the timber.

Each length of timber has to be marked and cut in exactly the same manner.

The poles are then permanently fixed to the stands by being bolted above the joint. Any method of fastening will do, but it is most important that the whole is rigid when completed.

THE POLES

Any ordinary round pole will do and should be some 4in. to 5in. diameter. I would recommend them to be some 10ft. long, but keep in mind that the whole must not be too heavy for one person to carry. Whatever the length decided upon, all the cavaletti should be **exactly** the same length.

REQUIREMENTS OF GOOD CAVALETTI

The important points of good cavaletti are:

1] . . . each should be an exact replica of the other so that one will stand easily and firmly upon the other;

2] . . . standing the cavaletti on its bottom, side or top will place the pole at a different height;

3] . . . each should be light enough to be carried easily by one person.

4] . . . there should be no sharp edges or points on the finished stands. A few strokes with a rasp will overcome this.

5] . . . the poles should be fixed rigidly to the ends so that each cavaletti is a complete unit, ready to be jumped wherever or however it is laid down.

FIRST JUMPING LESSONS

Before a class does any jumping, I have always made a point of demonstrating why the rider should lean forward each time the horse jumps.

Most horses are a little short of being eight feet [2.4m] long and so when dealing with even a very small jump such as a single pole, the horse has to give his body quite a hard push just to get his length over. It is to deal with this 'push' or jerk, that we advise *be sure you lean forward if you want to stay with your horse.*

Should the rider be sitting upright as the horse jumps, he will find himself being 'left behind' as the saddle shoots forward without him. The rider's seat will be taken forward with the saddle but his shoulders will be left behind — and if the jump is big enough he will be lucky to avoid a fall.

DEMONSTRATION

To demonstrate what happens, I let my whip represent the rider and my hand represent the horse. I balance the upright whip on my hand — and let the pupils see that if I move my hand suddenly in any direction, the upright whip will fall in the opposite direction to the thrust.

I continue: "And to make sure you won't be late in leaning forward, I ask you **to perch on — or over — your stirrups** when approaching a jump: lean forward with your seat just clear of the saddle". [Prior to the 20th Century riders leaned back when jumping; this too, avoids being 'left behind' when the horse jumps: Chapter 1 tells why the 'forward seat' was adopted.]

The illustrations that follow show Mr Keith Guster, Chief Instructor of the Dressage Club of South Australia, at work with a class that spreads over four or five weekends. It is most unusual for Keith to have a fall at his jumping classes, and the pictures show how from the lowest and simplest jump settings, both horses and their riders come to enjoy their jumping.

CAVALETTI NOT RECOMMENDED FOR BUILDING BIG JUMPS
But I don't recommend you to use cavaletti for building big fences. If hit hard, they will sometimes go with the horse, get tangled with his legs and there's a risk of bringing the horse down.

☆   ☆   ☆

Now let's see cavaletti at work: 'one picture is worth a thousand words' . . .

Fig. 47
Having walked over a single cavaletti without resistance, the horse is then asked to walk over a number, one after the other, still set at their lowest level and some 4 ft [1.2 m] apart. This teaches the horse to watch where he places his feet and to flex his limbs.
The expression on the horse's face leads me to wonder if he is thinking: "How silly can they be? Walking over all these things when we could quite easily go around them . . ."

Fig. 48
Trotting over cavaletti spaced at some 5 ft [1.5 m] with the poles set at their centre height. This particular exercise asks for a greater mobility of the horse's shoulders and limbs.
The more a horse is able to flex his joints the less he needs to lift his body when jumping. [The year the great English horse "Foxhunter" won the Olympic Games Show-jumping, movie films showed that his belly touched the rail of one jump but his legs were clear — he did not knock the rail down.]

Fig. 49
Cavaletti set at the top level and then cantered over make an excellent exercise for horse and rider. The horse learns to judge distance and place his feet — and to deal with difficulties when he meets them: and so too, does the rider. About 10 ft [3 m] between them at first but later on increases or decreases can be made to lengthen or shorten the stride.

Fig. 50
First horse and rider clear the double before tackling a change of direction. Later they are required to change direction within the very small square formed for the cavaletti — the squares start off quite large and then are made smaller — or larger — to give variety.

148

Fig. 51
Horse and rider are given much practice at these low level obstacles, the horse becoming more supple and flexible, with easy smooth changes of direction, before being faced with more difficult obstacles. The rider is learning control and judgement.

Fig. 52
Jumps are kept wide and low until the horse learns he can be in trouble if he takes off too soon — too far from the fence. Instructor Keith Guster is clearly WITH his pupils.

Fig. 53
As the judgement of horse and rider improves, the height is raised and by this time the rider is keeping nicely in contact with her horse's mouth.

Fig. 54
Later on, cavaletti are used to introduce horse and rider to cross-country work. Here we see two cavaletti set at the top of a small creek adjoining the Club grounds. Later on more will be placed at the top of the creek on the other side — and another at the bottom; other combinations will follow. I need hardly say both horse and rider are first made familiar with crossing the creek without jumps — "PREP..AR..ATION"!

[Photos: I. Roddie]

Fig. 55
A good jumping seat: the late Mr Franz Mairinger on A.J. Higgins' "Coronation". With shortened stirrups he perches close to his horse over the jump. Quiet contact is maintained throughout the leap and the rider is in complete control as he lands.

[Courtesy Mrs Higgins]

SHOW-JUMPING

EVOLUTION OF THE SHOW-JUMPING SEAT

I mentioned in Chapter 1 the discovery of the 'forward seat' in connection with racing — and jumping.

Although the racing seat has seen little change over the past fifty years, this is not so with the jumping seat. There have been notable changes in this since Caprilli's day. The original Italian seat was a military seat, which meant it had to be a general, all-purpose seat. It is still accepted as a good hunting or all-purpose seat and is ideal for long periods in the saddle, but for show-jumping and high jumping there have been considerable changes or developments.

Both the racing jockey and the show-jumping rider of today use a very short stirrup to allow them to take their knees as far forward as possible and all racing and jumping saddles are now cut forward to accommodate the knees when so advanced.

The shorter the stirrup, the further forward the rider can take his knees and the higher and further forward the saddle flaps need to extend. At the actual time of racing or jumping, the rider places his weight forward over the knees and in front of the stirrups. Throughout the actual jump the show-jumping rider does not touch the seat of his saddle — he perches or stands as far forward over his knees as he possibly can — at least during the first part of the actual jump.

As horse and rider reach the take-off point, the horse lifts his forelegs towards the top of the fence — rears up on his hind legs — and at the same time and while the horse's hindfeet are still on the ground — his rider does something similar from the saddle.

The rider is already perched well forward over his knees and, depending on the height and type of jump, he now stands up and stretches forward and up along the horse's neck until in many cases the rider's head is actually above the horse's ears for a brief moment.

THE HORSE "JUMPS UP TO THE RIDER"

At first this style was adopted by only a few riders. Among themselves, leading riders spoke of this standing and reaching up as "the horse jumps up to the rider". As the horse lifts his forehand and while his hinds are still on the ground, the rider stands up — and forward — in the saddle. [See Fig. 56.]

During the first part of the leap, the rider, by thrusting forward and up from his stirrups, is actually travelling faster than his horse. In the second part of the leap — the thrust of the horse's hindquarters off the ground — it is the horse that is travelling faster. On slow-motion film we plainly see both horse and rider clearing the fence with the horse 'catching up with his rider'. Both horse and rider are moving forward, with the horse moving a little faster and so catching up with the rider — the horse **is** 'jumping up to the rider'.

Fig. 56
"THE HORSE JUMPS UP TO THE RIDER": the horse's hind feet have just left the ground and he is in the act of thrusting forward to catch up with his rider over the jump. The rider, Mr Geoff Evans, on "Cygnet Rambler", is in full control on landing. This combination was very hard to beat. Before Geoff took him over, "Cygnet Rambler" did some of his early jumping at the Club grounds under his previous owner, Mr John Samuel-White. He was as notorious for his buckjumping as he later became famous for his show-jumping and buckjumping combined!

[Courtesy Mrs L. Evans
from "The Chronicle"]

NOT FOR THE BEGINNER

But this is for the very advanced horseman and fences of much greater height — when the gain of the smallest fraction of an inch in height is sought. The less experienced rider should FIRST learn to control his body and keep his seat very close to the saddle.

The rich show-jumping prizes of today lead riders to take many risks in the show-ring. The successful rider spends much time in preparing his horse for the demands that will later be made on him.

When schooling his horse, the more experienced rider will see that his horse gains judgement and confidence and agility, not by attempting fences of greater and greater height, but by the use of many varied jumps of lesser height.

To succeed in today's show-jumping, a horse needs to be well-schooled on the flat, and he needs to be physically prepared for the task to be asked of him. He should not be asked to jump higher or wider jumps than he has been prepared for until he is experienced — and confident. A "thinking" rider will raise his cap to the judge and retire his young horse from a competition when he feels the jumps warrant it. The knowledgeable onlooker will approve his decision.

START LOW AND CONTINUE LOW

Many years ago a prominent show-jumping rider from England was visiting our Dressage Club grounds where we had a class jumping cavaletti — which were then new to Australia.

A disparaging remark about their height was passed by another onlooker, and I replied: "This is where we all start — low at first, and only becoming higher as horses and riders gain confidence and judgement."

I well remember how our overseas visitor turned to me and said: "I couldn't agree with you more. I COULDN'T agree with you more! When I'm training a jumper for myself I follow much the same course. Start low and continue low, and gradually bring the horse to 3 ft. 6 inches. I never jump my own young horses over more than that height until they jump in the show-ring."

☆   ☆   ☆

Aim for confidence and familiarity with all types of fences, and at all angles; then, when your horse meets a bigger jump, he deals with it without question.

I don't propose to say more than this about show-jumping, for it has to be learnt by experience — the hard way.

☆   ☆   ☆

TO SUM UP

Versatility is the outstanding characteristic of the cavaletti. They can be used alone, in sets or in combinations, or with other fences.

Simple and easy to construct, they should be light enough to be carried easily by one person.

Each cavaletti should stand firmly upon the other.

The poles are fixed rigidly to the stands, and depending upon how each stand is set, three different height levels may be obtained.

There should be no sharp edges.

When about to jump, riders should lean or perch forward over their knees.

Many low jumps of varying widths serve better in the training field than jumps of greater height.

The horse should be thoroughly prepared, both physically and mentally, for the demands that will later be made of him in the show-jumping arena.

CHAPTER 25

INTRODUCING A PONY TO POLO

Difficulties that may be met;
Sore mouths;
To stop quickly;
Slow chukkas;
Introducing stick and ball;
'Forward';
Women players more than hold their own;
Capt. J.J. Pearce: advice.

☆   ☆   ☆

YOUR FIRST PONY

I have received several requests to include a chapter on polo in this, my third book.

Although I played polo for years both in India and in Australia, I certainly do not think I would be justified in holding myself up as an authority on the game — I can't even remember the rules at present — and before you begin you should be well aware of all the rules of the game.

But — when it comes to handling difficult polo-ponies, I might be able to help some of those riders asking for advice.

FIRST, I would advise a beginner *not* to start off with ponies that have already proved difficult. If an experienced player has given up with a pony, such a pony is almost sure to prove more difficult with an inexperienced player.

However, as you may have bought — or been loaned — such a pony, let's look at the difficulties you are most likely to meet, in the hope that I can help you BOTH.

155

SORE MOUTHS COME FIRST

It was a polo pony that began my study of bits. Do read every word of my first book, "HORSE CONTROL AND THE BIT", for much of what is written there I learned from correcting ponies of great value — first-class and expensive ponies that had 'gone wrong' with a new owner. In almost every case the pony had good reason to expect excessive pain from the bit once he was in the game.

Such ponies may, and often do, finish up as bolters or rearers. Bolting of course does not make sense: it isn't sense, it is desperation. And a desperation that often pays a dividend, as many riders stop pulling when they find they are on a bolting horse.

Other ponies repeatedly rear — stand up on their hind legs — and you cannot persuade or coerce them into forward movement.

TO CORRECT A REARER

To rear, a horse must be stationary. For if you can make him go forward, he has to put all four feet to the ground.

In polo, the cause of this trouble is usually a bad or painful bit AND THIS HAS FIRST TO BE ATTENDED TO.

Then the pony has to be given the "Go Forward Lesson" Ch. 10, "HORSE CONTROL — THE YOUNG HORSE, with particular attention to pp. 94 and 95. I won't repeat the instructions here, but I particularly recommend you to read the whole chapter and become completely at home with it.

TO STOP QUICKLY, A PONY MUST CHANGE HIS BALANCE

Sheer thoughtlessness often leads to the rearing that sometimes occurs on the playing field. Only too often, by the time a young pony goes forward as ordered on any occasion, the direction of the game has changed — and as soon as he has started to move the horse is stopped by the painful bit in the hands of a rider *who gives no thought* as to how the pony sees this agonising result of his obedience to the earlier order to go forward.

He, the pony, learns after a few experiences that to go forward leads **to much more pain** than the rider's whip or spurs if he does NOT go forward.

What in these circumstances can the horse think, except that he is being punished for going forward?

When riding a young or difficult pony always stop him gently — particularly if his mouth is sore or has been: whatever the cause.

Later on, he will understand that you have, for some reason, changed your mind and that you *now* want him to check or stop.

Remember — no animal can stop from forward movement without first changing its balance. Your polo pony needs a short light warning so that he can put his weight back. He is then in a position to change from his 'gallop on' to 'stop'.

THE MORE HE IS HURT THE LESS ATTENTION HE CAN GIVE TO THE NECESSARY CHANGE OF BALANCE. WITHOUT CHANGING HIS BALANCE HE CANNOT STOP QUICKLY.

Pain, particularly a sharp pain, is a distraction. Pain in this case distracts the pony from the stop the rider has asked of him.

THE GAME

I should perhaps mention somewhere that there is no height limit to a polo 'pony', for the usual definition of 'pony' does not apply in polo: a 16-hand horse qualifies as a polo-pony.

A 'chukka', to those who don't play, is a 'round'. Like a game of tennis — and others — a polo match is divided into parts: six chukkas to the game.

SLOW CHUKKAS

All clubs provide a number of 'slow chukkas' when necessary, in order to give members a chance to introduce new ponies to the game.

Fast galloping is frowned upon in a slow chukka, particularly when a green pony is close at hand. Young ponies should be introduced to the game in these slow chukkas, and I need hardly say that a lot of work has to be done on the pony well before he goes on to the ground while a game, slow or not, is on.

Before you take him on to the ground, check to see that your pony has a comfortable and mild bit in his mouth. Study 'HORSE CONTROL AND THE BIT' and learn that a horse's jaw is quite different from what has been accepted and taught for hundreds of years: every polo player should read the facts and recommendations set out. A snaffle, for instance, is quite out of place in some mouths — and hands.

Use the mildest bit available, and use it gently — particularly when introducing the pony to the game.

PREP . . AR . . ATION

The pony should have been 'broken to stick and ball' and introduced to several other things before even entering a slow chukka. "Prep . . ar . . ation", as one of the great riders of yesteryear, Capt. J.J. Pearce, used to drawl, "Prep . . ar . . ation".

The thing most likely to frighten a young pony in even a slow chukka is the sight of another pony being ridden towards him, and the rider of that pony perhaps swinging his polo stick.

This situation will continually recur, and like so many other things it must be introduced to the pony before he goes into any game or practice. "Prep .. ar .. ation"!

Two riders can practise this at a walk at first; and on any piece of ground. Each rides towards the other to pass — stick in hand perhaps — and each rider passes the other "stick hand to stick hand". At first do this a good distance apart, and if you carry polo sticks, keep them still.

If either pony is frightened, keep it up at a walk until he realises it is safe to walk on, and he goes straight past the other. Yes: 'safe': for a pony will often try to shy off to his left and the rider, endeavouring to keep him straight, will appear to the pony to be *attempting to run him right into the approaching pony and that rider's stick.*

Remember your pony has not the slightest idea of what lies ahead of him. "Don't hurry. It takes longer!"

Neither rider should attempt to hit at a ball until both horses can be walked straight through without attempting to move away. When eventually a ball is used, and only after the youngster is broken to the stick, it should be given a light tap only . . . and towards the rider's rear.

BREAKING TO STICK AND BALL

I need hardly say 'breaking to the stick' comes before 'breaking to the ball'.

If we are about to introduce the stick to the pony — THAT IS NOT WHAT WE START OFF DOING. We first PREPARE him for the sight of the moving stick.

Let the pony, if he is a nervous type, become accustomed to seeing your right fore-arm making small circular movements — and repeat this until he takes absolutely no notice of it.

Next, begin to carry a short stick, about 3 ft. or a metre in length. Hold it up your arm out of sight and then, little by little, let it project out of your hand. When the pony shows he is ready for it, let the stick touch his neck occasionally and later on, all being well, touch him behind the saddle, off-side.

By this time he is almost as good as broken to a stick, and you can start holding a full-length polo stick in your 'stick hand'. Hold it short at first, then gradually let it play out as you did the shorter stick. Use one without a head to it at first: when he accepts this, let the pony see it on his near side occasionally. Don't go any further with any of this work until the pony takes absolutely no notice of a headless stick on either side of him.

Don't hurry: and don't go any further in this or in any other matter until the horse is well over any fear he may at first show. So much depends upon the individual pony — a day or so is plenty with some; a couple of weeks or even months for others.

Remember the advice of the colt-breaker, Danny Fitzgerald: "Don't hurry. It takes longer." Do not hurry . . . but think, think, THINK . . . and always notice how the pony is behaving.

STICK-SHY — AN INDIAN POLO-PONY

An experience I had in India might prove interesting, and helpful too, in this matter.

When I was serving near Poona, India, in about 1922, my C.O. had arranged to be given first choice of two ponies of a whole shipload of horses then about due to arrive in Bombay. All had been ridden before leaving Australia.

In due course the first of the two selected horses arrived at the Regiment's Riding School for me to begin his education for polo. The horse proved to be very quiet to ride [many of them were anything but!]. However, I had not been on his back very long before I felt sure I could feel an unevenness in his trot.

After a while I sent him back to his stable as being slightly lame. Neither the Regimental Vet. nor I could see the lameness, although I could definitely *feel* it when mounted. To cut the sad story short, the lameness worsened with time, and the horse eventually had to be 'put down'. One of the Major's expensive horses was a "dead" loss.

Worse was to follow for, notwithstanding every care, the second horse, a thoroughbred, turned out to be incredibly stick-shy.

I tried everything — but he continued to jump about at the slightest movement of a polo-stick in his rider's hand. At the end of several months he showed not the slightest improvement in this matter, although in all other training matters he showed great promise.

Every move I knew, I tried; and I even went to the extent of hanging about twenty sticks in the animal's stall so that he couldn't move without touching some of them. It produced no improvement. It was a most dejected Major who stood in the School watching almost every day.

That horse gave me many sleepless hours; and in one such period I remember telling myself: "I've done everything but hit him with a stick . . . everything but . . ."

Suddenly I was wide awake. He HAD NEVER FELT a polo stick in a rider's hand.

When I rode him early that next morning, a touch on the neck with the stick quite high up near my hand, brought about an amazing change.

Before that day's work was over, I could swing the stick without the pony showing more than a nice interest. His stick-shying was over.

Before I finished his work for the day, in came the Major. He was both excited and delighted to see the horse ignoring the stick and completely over his trouble.

"Excellent, Roberts, excellent! However did you bring it about?" . . . I made the mistake of telling him.

His face dropped — and he said: "You hit him with the stick? You HIT him with the stick?? YOU SHOULD NEVER HIT A POLO PONY WITH A POLO STICK. YOU SHOULD *KNOW* THAT!" You can't win, I reflected.

Anyway, the stick-shying corrected, this excellent thoroughbred went on to become a first class polo-pony and proved to be very fast. No other pony in a game could stay with him in a run for the ball.

☆   ☆   ☆

Some years later when the Regiment was about to return to England and I about to take my discharge and move to Australia, I backed him at very long odds when the Major decided to race him at Kirkee: an 'all-unknown' on the racetrack.

The 100-odd pounds the pony won for me helped set me up eventually in South Australia as a bee-keeper, in 1924. One hundred pounds was a lot of money in those days. I backed him, the 'unknown', at 10 to 1!

INTRODUCING THE PONY TO A BALL

The pony is not ready to be introduced to a ball while he is in any degree 'stick-shy' — and even then, you don't start off hitting at the ball.

Our first goal is to get the pony accustomed to the sound of the ball being struck. Take an old stick and ride away off the polo ground and start tapping at any small stones you may see on the ground where you are riding. Just the lightest of taps and very little stones at first, and usually in a very short time the sound will not worry or even interest your pony.

Knock the stones to your rear at first so that the pony won't see them move. Later on, when he shows he is ready, begin to knock an occasional one somewhat forward and to his off-front. We want him to come to associate sound and movement from the point of the sound, and I need hardly say that when we actually start to hit a ball we follow the same procedure.

Next, throw a number of balls out on the ground. Let the pony get used to seeing them there and in due course you can occasionally lean towards them as if you were going to hit one. But don't actually strike it. Let the stick-head pass over the ball.

Always hit to the rear at first. When the pony shows you he is ready for it, tap the ball a yard or two to his right front — away from him.

Some ponies do not need all these precautions; but why take unnecessary chances? If you have the time, why not take advantage of it.

You can start these things long before you are thinking of hitting a ball.

PONY'S TAIL CAN CAUSE TROUBLES

You will also notice that almost every polo pony has his tail plaited and then tied up in order *to avoid getting the stick caught up in it* when hitting to the front. In colder climates, where flies are perhaps not such a worry to horses, the tails are sometimes cut to dock-length.

A long tail can be a real menace when hitting at a ball in a polo-match. Be most careful not to let your stick be caught up in your pony's tail when you are just schooling . . . it can set him back weeks.

See that his tail is plaited before you start hitting at a ball.

"FORWARD . . . FORWARD . . ."

It is most essential that you have grasped the essentials of the "Go Forward Lesson". Your pony must fully understand what your legs and your whip mean. This cannot be taught on the polo ground — read again Ch. 10 of 'HORSE CONTROL — THE YOUNG HORSE' pp. 86-98.

You can do nothing with a horse until you can make him go forward. *A pony is not ready for polo if he doesn't answer your legs, not only immediately but as if it were compulsive to do so.* To be able to enforce "Go Forward" is a first essential in all horse control.

Before World War II a Mr O.V. Roberts of Clare, South Australia, was a frequent rider in polo matches held in Adelaide and a first-class player and horseman I found him to be. When I began playing there, having the same surname we were always referred to by our initials only, just O.V. or T.A. Our surnames and our common interests drew us together and we frequently had very good talks after which I would not hesitate to say 'thanks', for I found I could learn much from him.

I was almost always on a very good pony, although usually one that had started to go wrong and had come to me for correction. The very expensive but 'gone wrong' pony I was riding at this time was just beginning to come good again. Nobody pays big four-figure sums [pounds in those days — not dollars, remember] for a pony unless it is very good and has proved it.

This pony, as soon as he came to know me, began to be most co-operative.

When he found that the bit *was not to be so painful*, he would stop at great speed — and when asked to do so would turn about and be off at great speed again. When stopping, he would bring his hindquarters under, where they were ideally

161

placed for the halt, turn, and gallop-on that usually followed.

I told O.V. that he wouldn't be able to live with the pony once it had full confidence in me — but O.V. only answered with a smile: "Time will show".

It was only a few weeks later that I was able to demonstrate my point. O.V. and I had been passing in opposite directions, stick-hand to stick-hand as usual, when a change in the game occurred and I had to stop, turn about and then overtake him to have any chance of getting the ball.

"I'll beat you to it!" I called to a laughing O.V. as I passed him, going in the opposite direction. And I was able to do just that — to his astonishment.

First, you have to establish an understanding with your pony. Then — with a first-class pony as this one was — make your aids as smoothly and gently as possible . . . and he will put every effort into the movement he knows is required.

Pain distracts: and a pony just cannot carry out the movement if he is hurt too much.

WOMEN PLAYERS MORE THAN HOLD THEIR OWN AT POLO

From Adelaide's "The Advertiser": 50 Years Ago: Jan. 5, 1930 — "Two teams of girls opposed each other in what is believed to be the first polo match played in South Australia between two teams consisting entirely of women."

One more important item. Polo is at least one game in which ladies are allowed to take part and this has been so for many years. Two quite young girls [Mary and Elizabeth Teesdale-Smith if memory serves me right] played regularly at Birkalla Polo Ground when I was playing there, and were at least up into the top half of players. Their ponies were all bred, broken-in, and schooled by members of the family.

Light and well-mounted, the girls usually played as No. 1 and No. 2, and so their role was "attack".

I always remember them playing *a good 'position' game: WHERE THEY SHOULD BE, THAT'S WHERE YOU WOULD FIND THEM.*

Polo, above all things, is a team game.

Mary Teesdale-Smith was also one of a team that played against Mount Crawford, and after the War she made a name in cross-country. She hunted regularly and won several points-to-point — on different horses in different years.

Good horsemanship — and good polo — is not a matter of strength or sex.

Fig. 57
LADIES, TOO, PLAY POLO . . . Mary Teesdale-Smith: and note the quite relaxed expression of the pony. She is using a Pelham bit which most horses find more comfortable in polo. Their horses all seemed to ENJOY their polo.

✪   ✪   ✪

CAPT. J.J. PEARCE

Before closing this chapter I would like to pass on two items of very sound advice on riding in either a game or when practising. The advice comes from the late Capt. J.J. Pearce, who stressed these two points in ALL his teachings:

1] Check or steady your pony before you hit the ball.
2] When you are about to strike the ball, lower your bridle hand on to your pony's neck.

I found this second item most interesting — and valuable.

163

The two warnings amount to:
- ★ CHECK OR STEADY YOUR PONY AS YOU NEAR THE BALL,
- ★ AND TAKE A SIMPLE PRECAUTION AGAINST HANGING ON TO HIS MOUTH.

I learnt a lot from Jimmy Pearce.

TO SUM UP

Riders about to commence playing polo are advised not to begin with a pony that has already proved to be difficult.

Mouth troubles are very common in ponies that become difficult to play. Such ponies sometimes turn to rearing or bolting.

'HORSE CONTROL AND THE BIT' is recommended reading to riders with a horse that has become difficult to stop; and 'HORSE CONTROL — THE YOUNG HORSE' to those with horses that turn to rearing.

Slow chukkas are provided by polo clubs to introduce young ponies to the game, but much preparation has to be given a pony before attempting such games. The pony should be 'broken to a stick' before any attempt is made to hit at a ball.

The horse has first to be accustomed to having to pass, head-on, another pony passing in the opposite direction, with perhaps that rider swinging a polo-stick. He has then to be introduced to the moving ball.

No matter what the horse is wanted for, he will be useless unless he goes forward upon demand. To go forward in all circumstances is a first essential.

During a game, ponies are repeatedly stopped immediately after having obeyed the rider and galloped forward. If the pain of spurs or whip is immediately followed by a very sharp pain from the bit, the young pony often becomes hopelessly confused.

A pony galloping forward has to change his balance before he can stop quickly: and the more he is hurt with the bit the less attention he can give to the necessary change of balance.

Women players do much better than just hold their own at polo, and have proved their quality over the years.

Read again the comments of the late Capt. J.J. Pearce: his advice is invaluable.

CHAPTER 26

SAFETY IN THE SADDLE — AND OUT OF IT

A foot caught in the stirrup iron: what to do;
Stirrups — and boots; Stirrup releases;
'Tidy' leathers;
Concussion or a blow to the head;
Always wear a helmet;
Riding through water;
Avoid riding along steep slopes;
Greasy roads.

YOUR FOOT CAUGHT IN THE STIRRUP IRON — WHAT TO DO

It might be a good idea to pass on again what to do if you should fall and find or fear that your foot is trapped in a stirrup iron:

KICK IMMEDIATELY AT THE **IRON** WITH THE FOOT THAT IS FREE.

I have never seen both feet caught up.

It requires only a slight knock on the iron with the foot that is free. Doing so will almost surely immediately free the foot that is trapped.

Instructors should all make a point of teaching this safety-measure to their pupils, and all parents should show it to their children. I need hardly say that if you do demonstrate it to others, see that the stirrup or leather is attached to a rail or other fixture — and not to a live horse! If you can demonstrate it at home, the stirrup iron needs to be hung only about three feet [1 m] from the ground.

Whenever I have felt myself parting company with any horse, the first thing I think is: "Are my feet free?" They usually are. My next thought is to hold the horse and not let him gallop off.

BUT FIRST AND FOREMOST — BE READY TO KNOCK THE STIRRUP **IRON** WITH THE FOOT YOU HAVE FREE.

"SAFETY" STIRRUPS

Just calling a stirrup a 'Safety Stirrup' decides many people to buy stirrups that I consider are anything but safe. I feel I should say something about some of them.

For instance I cannot recommend any safety stirrups that have to be fastened on to any particular side of the saddle, for it is much too easy to attach

165

them to the *wrong side*. This is particularly the case with an inexperienced person — and what was designed to increase the safety of the rider might well do the opposite.

The same with stirrup irons that require the foot to be placed in them from a certain side. They may facilitate the release of the foot if they are first fitted on the correct side of the saddle and then the foot placed in as recommended — and kept there. But we all 'lose our stirrups' on occasion, and when we take them again we can, and often do, put a foot in from the wrong side. What is intended to be a safety design can then become more risky than the normal stirrup iron. I cannot recommend any such stirrup as being safer than the ordinary iron.

Professional horsemen. You may have noticed that jumping riders, stockmen, jockeys, etc., seldom if ever use any type of 'safety' stirrup iron. Surely they would do so if they believed in them?

I recommend: *do not buy a stirrup iron just because it is called safe.* No doubt there are safety stirrups available — but just calling them 'Safety Stirrups' will not necessarily make them safe.

SIZE OF STIRRUP IRON

Stirrup irons that are much larger than the foot to go in them are a danger to be avoided. If much too big, the whole boot can slip through the iron when the rider is unsteady in the saddle and result in the rider being 'dragged' in the event of a fall. The rider's only hope then lies in the stirrup leather detaching from the saddle-dee — which we deal with later.

I noticed in a recent Canadian magazine, "The Corinthian", that the heels of all their riding boots are now required to be a certain height. Low heels can slip through most stirrup irons. This is one reason why most riding boots are made with high heels.

LIGHT STIRRUP IRONS

An excessively light stirrup iron can be very dangerous too, as very light irons tend to cling to the boot if the rider should fall from his horse. I advise — avoid very light stirrup irons.

STIRRUP IRONS OF SOFT METAL

Avoid, too, any stirrup iron made of soft metal. Such irons have been known to flatten around the foot when horse and rider fall with the horse's weight on the rider's foot [see Fig. 58]. Your only hope in the event of the horse galloping off and dragging you when he gets up — is that the stirrup leather will pull off at the saddle stirrup-dee.

I advise, in the strongest terms: do not ride with stirrups of soft metal. Keep to stainless steel or steel.

Fig. 58
"Stirrups of soft metal are not to be recommended." Should horse and rider fall on to the rider's foot while the foot is still in the stirrup, the weight of the horse can bend the stirrup as it did with the iron shown here. The stirrup shown is stamped: "SOLID NICKLE".

RIDING BOOTS THAT HAVE TO BE RE-SOLED

Another safety matter. If you have your riding boots resoled at any time, see that the new sole is fixed on so as not to form a ridge that will engage or catch on the tread of the iron. The part of the boot from under the instep should be nailed on so that IT OVERLAPS the new sole.

When so placed, it will not form a ridge that will catch on the tread of the iron: this is a most important safety precaution.

The usual manner of fitting a new sole to a boot or shoe leaves a ridge that can hold the stirrup iron in a fall [see also p. 33, "HORSE CONTROL — THE YOUNG HORSE" for other safety matters].

STIRRUP RELEASES

Most saddle stirrup-dees [the dees on the saddle-tree around which the stirrup leather is buckled] are designed to allow the stirrup leather to pull free if a rider is being 'dragged'.

Putting the free end of the stirrup-leather under a surcingle or through a slit in the saddle-flap will completely nullify this safety device on the saddle. *Don't ever do this.*

The ends of the stirrup leathers must NOT BE FIXED TO THE SADDLE OR SADDLE-FLAP in any manner likely to negative the saddle-maker's so carefully conceived saddle stirrup-dee.

"TIDY" STIRRUP LEATHERS

Watch to see that no free or 'running end' of a stirrup leather is tucked under the surcingle or through a slit in the saddle-flap *to get it neatly out of the way.*

Most of the best saddles have a keeper sewn on the saddle-flap into which the free end of the leather can be tucked away. But see that it is sewn on to the saddle-flap WITH ONLY A FEW STITCHES — so it will break free if the rider is in danger of being dragged.

I much prefer the older type of keeper: the modern keepers are often too *strong*: be sure yours will break free if ever it should become necessary.

PACKING AND STUFFING OF THE SADDLE

If not carefully done, the packing or stuffing of a saddle can make the safety device on the saddle stirrup-dee quite ineffective.

Too much stuffing under the saddle-dee not only makes the stirrup leather difficult to get on to the saddle-dee, but *can make it almost impossible to pull off* if ever the rider falls and his foot is trapped in the stirrup.

Children run the greatest risk with this defect, being light in weight. The saddler can correct the fault in a very short while — but remember, if the stirrup leather is very difficult to get under the saddle-dee it will not drag off as it should. This check should be made when the saddle is on the horse [or pony] and when the girth is tight.

The opposite can also be a danger. Too little packing can allow the leather to pull off too easily with some types of saddle-dee.

Check your saddle — and your children's saddles — for safety in this matter.

☆   ☆   ☆

CONCUSSION OR A BLOW TO THE HEAD

We have travelled now to falls, and I feel this might be a good time to mention the action to be taken if anyone should fall and strike their head — or be kicked on the head.

A blow to the skull should never be taken lightly: NEVER.

I had such a fall in hospital a while ago, while strapped into a wheelchair. My wheelchair fell with me and added its weight to mine — and my head struck the floor a most resounding blow.

The blow was immediately treated as an emergency — possible concussion. Doctors were called, the skull examined, and they ordered an icepack to be strapped on to my forehead immediately over the site of the blow.

MINIMISE THE EFFECTS. If anyone, adult or child, suffers a sharp blow to the head, however caused, get them to a doctor or better still call a doctor to them, as soon as possible.

On no account just lay them down or let them go to sleep. Hospital treatment is recommended, but if possible get a doctor to see the injury. He will advise on the action to be taken. If the patient is allowed to fall asleep, there is a strong chance he will not regain consciousness.

My icepack consisted of crushed ice in a plastic bag. The plastic container stopped the melting ice dripping all over my head and face, and the ice checked the likely inflammation and bruising.

If you have to move the sufferer before a doctor sees him, do so most gently and cautiously. I had my fall in a hospital — and even so, every precaution was taken.

ANY SHARP BLOW TO THE HEAD IS MOST SERIOUS, OR CAN BE. GET A DOCTOR OR RING HIM OR A HOSPITAL FOR ADVICE OR HELP IMMEDIATELY. IN THE MEAN- TIME, DO NOT LET THE INJURED PERSON GO TO SLEEP.

Do not take a chance with any blow to the head. Always treat it as being serious . . . *and never let the injured person "sleep it off".*

ALWAYS WEAR PROTECTIVE HEADGEAR

ALWAYS . . . and a chin strap. Of course, you may never need it — but let me tell you of a splendid young rider who once neglected to do so.

The Helen Junge Memorial Trophy: Helen ran a very good riding school for children at her home and ALWAYS used a skull-cap — and insisted on her pupils doing so too — always. Then one evening, just for once, she broke her own rule. She had a quiet gentle pony to move a short distance to the stables. She jumped up on it bareback — and without her cap. The pony stumbled and almost fell to its knees on the way — throwing Helen on to her head. She never regained consciousness and died two days later.

The Dressage Club of South Australia, to which she belonged, knew Helen would like her lapse to be a warning — and so presented the Memorial Trophy to the Adelaide Royal Show for annual competition.

We urge all riders to wear an approved skull cap with a chin strap — even though you may never need it.

☆   ☆   ☆

RIDING THROUGH WATER

The following is an item of some ten years ago from "The South Australian Rider", the magazine of the Dressage Club of South Australia.

> **"All cross-country riders** should be warned not to enter water of a depth of approximately 18" [0.5 m] or more at a fast pace.
> The water holds the horse's legs — but his body . . . and the rider . . . go on."

I always think a true incident adds point to instruction or advice.

When I was about 16 years old — and in the British Army — I was out riding with four other boys of about the same age. We knew the stream we were approaching was shallow, and too wide to jump — but when one lad shouted: "Last one over is mad" . . . well!

We learnt that lesson the hard way. It was a bitterly cold day, too.

AVOID RIDING **ALONG** STEEP SLOPES

If a horse slips while he is on a steep slope, his feet almost always slip downwards — down the slope. If the horse is sideways-on, he will slip on to his side *and he cannot recover his feet* from his narrow base. He is unable to get his feet under his weight — or his weight over his feet.

If headed straight down the slope, no harm results when the horse's forelegs slip, for his hinds are following and he just slides down instead of stepping down. If his hinds slip, they too slide downward — and the horse, being on his long base, merely sits down without losing his feet.

The Italian Cavalry would give the liveliest demonstrations of riding down slopes in days past . . . with their Alps they really had to know how to deal with steep slopes — straight down.

SLIPPING ON A "GREASY" ROAD

I might add here: avoid riding along a slippery road, *especially if it has a definite side-slope.*

A horse finds it most difficult to keep on his feet on any slippery **side** slope. I advise: "Get off the road — or ride in the gutter".

TO SUM UP

If there is any danger of you parting company with your horse, make sure your feet are free of the stirrup irons.

If your foot should be caught in an iron and there is danger of being 'dragged', BE READY TO KNOCK THE STIRRUP IRON WITH THE FOOT YOU HAVE FREE.

Just calling a stirrup iron a "Safety Stirrup" does not necessarily make it safe. Check all features and see if they can be relied upon under all circumstances.

Avoid stirrup-irons that are very much larger than the boot that is to go in them. If the foot can pass right through the stirrup when a rider is falling, the rider might well be 'dragged'.

Avoid very light stirrup-irons, for they tend to cling to the rider's boot if he falls from the saddle.

Stirrup irons made of soft metal can imprison the foot when a horse falls with all his weight on the foot and stirrup iron.

If riding boots have to be re-soled, be sure that the new sole is put on so as not to make a ridge that could engage the iron in a fall and so prevent the foot leaving the iron.

Almost all saddles are made with stirrup-dees that aim to release the stirrup when the rider falls and his foot is trapped in the iron. Check that all such fittings are in good condition — so that they will neither release the stirrup too easily nor fail to release if a light weight, such as a child, is hanging from the stirrup.

Never pass the loose end of a stirrup leather under a surcingle or anything else that will not release the stirrup should the rider fall.

If anyone receives a sharp blow to the head, treat it as being dangerous and call for medical help immediately. NEVER TAKE A BLOW TO THE HEAD LIGHTLY . . . NEVER. Call a doctor immediately and keep the injured person still, if that is possible. Do not, on any account, let him go to sleep. Call a doctor IMMEDIATELY.

Never ride into water of any depth at a fast pace; the water will hold the horse's legs but his body will continue on.

Avoid riding ALONG slopes. The horse can slip sideways, fall, and be unable to recover his feet until he reaches the bottom of the slope.

Always ride straight up or straight down steep slopes. So ridden, the horse may slip but he will not fall.

Avoid riding along roads that have a definite side-slope; the horse finds it difficult to keep on his feet on any slippery side-slope.

CHAPTER 27

FINAL ADVICE

LIGHT HANDS

Heavy hands make 'hard mouths';
Western riding;
The John Gniel Method of 'Educating';
Light hands: mounted and dismounted;
Effects of distraction;
Enjoy your riding.

HEAVY HANDS MAKE 'HARD MOUTHS'

Throughout this book I have stressed the importance of immediate obedience to light forward-driving aids — but so many riders have trouble in *stopping or checking* their horses that I feel I should say something about LIGHTNESS in response to bit and rein before I finish.

So often we hear a rider complain that his horse has a "hard mouth". By this he means that he thinks that his horse has little or no feeling in his mouth, and so is unable to feel light pressures of the bit. Nothing could be further from the truth.

Such riders fail to recognise that if a horse's mouth is hurt too much, the **excessive pain of the bit PREVENTS him** doing what is wanted of him.

I have said a good deal about the avoidance of force with the reins in each of my first books and I do not intend to repeat that advice. If you have a horse with a 'hard' mouth, do please go back and read the first nine pages of "HORSE CONTROL AND THE BIT". Read there how to avoid a 'hard' mouth. Also study what is said in Chapter 16 of this work, which deals with the 'Half Halt': read there what is said about preparing — or warning — the horse of a demand about to be made on him.

If **the rider** is heavy on the reins, how can the horse be light? It is the 'heavy hand' that makes what appears to be a 'hard' mouth. Pain from the bit is never a factor in good horse control.

☆   ☆   ☆

I would like to tell you of two methods that control a horse WITHOUT A BIT IN THE MOUTH . . . and I'll start with:

WESTERN RIDING

I must say that anyone who thinks it necessary to use the reins to hurt his

172

horse would be as impressed as I was when we accepted an invitation to visit the "WILLOMURRA QUARTER HORSE STUD" here in South Australia.

There, we saw a number of horses brought to an almost instant, an almost incredible, short stop WITH A COMPLETELY LOOSE REIN. Each horse put the same energy into every movement we asked of the rider, and not once was the rein even stretched. The horses all obeyed some slight movement of the rider's hand. All were ridden in a hackamore with the reins in one hand. No open mouths or heads in the air.

I mention Western Riding here in the hope of convincing riders who think otherwise . . . that hurting their horse's mouth is not only unnecessary but can be the *cause* of most of the resistances that lead to 'hard' mouths.

None of the horses had had more than three months' schooling. I recommend a visit to one of these reputable Quarter Horse studs if opportunity offers: not necessarily to take up Western Riding, but to learn that the horse does not have to be hurt to make him give all he possibly can to his rider.

It is not even necessary to have a bit in the horse's mouth at all.

I quote Franz Mairinger again, "If your horse is not doing what you want, it is because he does not KNOW what you want".

☆　　　☆　　　☆

Now let me tell you of:

THE JOHN GNIEL METHOD OF EDUCATION

Late in 1978 we received a letter from a professional horse-breaker — Mr John Gniel of 'Cooinda' Stud, Morgheboluc, Victoria.

Mr Gniel tells us he does not use a bit of any kind before a young horse is ridden, or even during his early rides. The success of his method is almost unbelievable, and I mention it here, with Western Riding, hoping that riders of "hard-mouthed" horses will look to other causes of the difficulty they experience in stopping their horses.

The Jeffery Method: John's breaking-in is based on the Jeffery Method [see Ch. 6, "HORSE CONTROL — THE YOUNG HORSE"]. To teach each horse to stop he uses the Jeffery ring-rope around the horse's neck. Using the ring-rope, John teaches each horse to stop and stand still while he is preparing it for the saddle, mounting, etc.

To control the horse's direction when mounted, he attaches the usual reins to each side of a well-adjusted halter — he uses no bit during the early rides.

Before mounting, he exchanges the long ring-rope for a short plaited leather one, with a 2" metal ring [see Fig. 59]. You will probably be as impressed as we

173

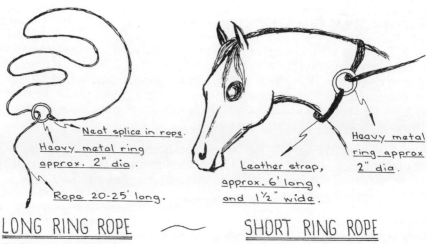

Neat splice in rope.
Heavy metal ring approx. 2" dia.

Rope 20-25' long.

Leather strap, approx. 6' long, and 1½" wide.

Heavy metal ring approx 2" dia.

LONG RING ROPE ～ SHORT RING ROPE

Fig. 59
Sketch by Penny Gniel [author of "Arabian Antics"]

were when we read in his letter: "The plaited leather must feel kinder to the horse, and I am sure that is why they are responding even better to this leather strap than to a short rope".

"With this mouthing method at no time do I ever have to pull in panic at the horse's mouth. Any pulling is done on the halter or the neck strap well before the bit is introduced. Consequently you will understand how we must finish up with a most responsive mouth — and a horse that carries itself naturally well."

A PULL ON THE NECK STRAP STOPS THE HORSE

"My clients are happy to hang a piece of rope or even a hay-band around the horse's neck as a safety strap when working the young horse. If at any time the horse gets frightened, a quick grab at the neck strap stops the horse and also helps the rider to stay in the saddle ... Giving the horse one lesson a day it usually takes me about two to three weeks to have him going happily at a walk, trot and canter and accepting everything in a calm and relaxed way. My clients include racehorse trainers, dressage riders, hacks and children's ponies. All seem to be extremely happy with the result — and I am happy to turn out happy horses."

I will say no more about the John Gniel Method of breaking-in — or educating. John and his wife, Penny, who is quite an artist, intend to publish a book on the method later. I only mention his system here, with Western Riding, in the hope of convincing readers that it is **HEAVY HANDS** that produce what appear to be 'hard' mouthed horses.

LIGHT HANDS — DISMOUNTED AND MOUNTED

Only too often a young horse is started on the road to a 'hard' mouth by the heavy use of rope or rein *before he is ridden.* [Chapter 4 of 'HORSE CONTROL —

174

THE YOUNG HORSE' deals with this matter of teaching a young horse to yield to a **lightly** drawn rope or rein. Either before or after mounting — force should never be used when teaching a youngster to lead, stop, turn, or step back.

A rider with good hands . . . a good horseman . . . always takes great care to see that his horse is given the opportunity to **avoid** being hurt. It is for all those who handle young horses to be light-handed at all times — mounted AND dismounted.

Think of the position of this truly willing animal that is so pleased to do what you want when he *knows* what you want. Think of his dreadful position when you — as many riders so often do — tear at his mouth: and he not knowing what to do about it.

THINK . . . THINK . . . THINK. The greatest compliment the Spanish Riding School in Vienna can give is to describe a horseman as a "Thinking Rider".

EFFECTS OF DISTRACTION

Before I leave this subject of lightness to the reins, I feel I must say something about the effects of distraction.

In Chapter 2 of "HORSE CONTROL AND THE BIT" I have dealt in detail with 'Causes and Results of Distraction'. Do go back and read it, for it is clear that if an ill-fitting saddle or anything else is hurting your horse it will distract his attention **from** your light rein-aids.

Some of the latest saddles of today are substituting plastic pads for the old stuffing: it can be produced in any thickness and any degree of firmness. Quite smooth and long-lasting, it is almost certain to be — with horsefloats [trailers] — the great innovation of the 20th Century. Time — and the horses' backs — will be the judge.

☆   ☆   ☆

Fig. 60

HE SITS 'TALL IN THE SADDLE': WESTERN RIDING
Mr Webb McKelvey of California, U.S.A., on his 9 year old mule "Blue". Note the alertness and attentiveness of "Blue" with one ear on the camera and the other showing attention to his rider. We cannot but notice the "weight down", the "body upright", and the light fingers of the rider [see pp. 47-51 "HORSE CONTROL — THE YOUNG HORSE" for Webb handling a wild station horse when visiting Australia].

So we come to the end of another book, and I hope it will help lead to a complete control of your horse. We should aim at a complete submission — but a buoyant submission in which the horse appears to take pleasure in showing how well he understands us.

Both you and your horse should enjoy your exercises, and should not only show enjoyment but you should make an attractive picture as you do so.

Old Captain Pearce, who at 84 claimed to be still learning, said on one occasion:

> "A good dressage horse steps out with a definite gaiety in his paces: as well as doing exactly what his rider asks of him."

J.J. called it: "élan".

I do hope what I have written will prove helpful whether you are interested in dressage . . . or hunting, polo, stockwork — or riding for your own pleasure.

☆   ☆   ☆

And what next? A fourth book . . .?

Every experience adds to one's knowledge — and most of the incidents I have in mind should prove both interesting and instructive . . . "HORSE CONTROL — REMINISCENCES"??

INDEX

179

INDEX

☆ *NOTES* ☆